INNER FREEDOM

INNER FREEDOM

How to Find and Dissolve Your Limiting Beliefs

Susanne Hunter, MD,
Registered Clinical Counsellor

Inner Freedom (revised edition)
Copyright © 2022, Susanne Hunter, MD, RCC

All rights reserved. No part of this publication may be reproduced, distributed, or transmitted in any form or by any means, including photocopying, recording, or other electronic or mechanical methods, without the prior written permission of the publisher, except in the case of brief quotations embodied in critical reviews and certain other noncommercial uses permitted by copyright law.

For permission requests, contact the publisher at:
susannehunter.counselling@gmail.com

Published by Healing Light Counselling

ISBN: 978-1-7776619-1-5 (softcover)

New reprint

Disclaimer: The information in this publication is drawn from the author's professional experience and is presented for educational purposes. She assumes no responsibility for outcomes as a result of using this information. This publication is not intended to be a substitute for a consultation with a medical or counselling professional.

Edited by Lesley Cameron

Page design, layout, and typesetting by
Jan Westendorp, katodesignandphoto.com

Hand-drawn illustrations by Bernadette Mertens-McAllister

Cover design by Angela Fraser

Cover photo © Shutterstock.com

Author photo by Amy Melious

CONTENTS

ABOUT THIS BOOK ix

INTRODUCTION xi

PART I: HOW BELIEFS AFFECT YOUR LIFE

Chapter 1
Where Do Your Beliefs Come From?
How Do They Become Ingrained in You? 5

Chapter 2
The Repeating Cycle:
Your Experiences Create Your Beliefs
Your Beliefs Create Your Experiences 25

Chapter 3
Reactions to a Limiting Belief 33

Chapter 4
Models of Limiting and Supportive Beliefs 39

Chapter 5
Feelings, Needs, and Strategies 47

Chapter 6
How Do You Find Your Beliefs? 61

Chapter 7
Beliefs about Your Feelings and Needs 75

Chapter 8
Our Beliefs Form Our Reality 87

Chapter 9
Getting Triggered 93

PART II: DISSOLVING YOUR LIMITING BELIEFS

Chapter 10
An Introduction to the Emotional Freedom Technique . . . 125

Chapter 11
The Basics of Tapping 129

Chapter 12
How to Tap to Dissolve Limiting Beliefs 135

Chapter 13
Examples of Tapping to Dissolve Limiting Beliefs 157

Chapter 14
Dos and Don'ts for Tapping. 171

Chapter 15
When a Recommended Action
   Promises to Fulfill Your Goals and Dreams 177

Chapter 16
Our Invisible Websites. 181

Chapter 17
How to Ask for What You Want
   from Abundance Instead of Scarcity 185

Chapter 18
The Power of "What If . . . " and
   How to Ask Questions That Move You Forward 193

Chapter 19
Getting Off the Cushion into Being Triggered 203

PART III: SHIFTING INTO ONENESS

Chapter 20
Three Realms and How
They Are Interlinked 209

Chapter 21
The Collective Invisible Website 219

Chapter 22
Our Experiences in the Three Realms
 and Separation Trauma 227

Chapter 23
Shifting Out of Separation into Oneness 235

Appendix 1: Universal Human Needs List 265

Appendix 2: Feelings List 266

Appendix 3: Road Map for Navigating the
 Trigger Response and Getting to the Gems 268

Appendix 4: Tapping Protocol for
 Dissolving Limiting Beliefs 270

Acknowledgements 273

About This Book

"I wish I had known THIS YEARS AGO." I heard those words over and over from clients when I shared with them the information you'll find in the book you're holding now. Hearing their words made me realize how valuable this information is for people and I wanted to make it more widely available. It motivated me to write this book.

We all feel stuck at times. I hope this book will help you when you feel stuck and want to move forward to live and experience whatever you are longing for in your life. This book can support you as you navigate your thoughts, feelings, patterns, and beliefs. It shows you very clear steps you can take to shift your beliefs and reality. It guides you in taking those steps in your own time, your own space, and the context of your own unique experience.

If you are a counsellor, coach, or therapist, this book can help support you as you guide your clients in finding and dissolving their limiting beliefs.

All the approaches, models, and paths in this book come from a wide knowledge base. I have been applying them for decades in my own life and guided others with them and through them in thousands of session hours.

The chapters are built on each other, so you might want to read the whole book through from start to finish first and then go back and apply the steps in a way that works for you personally. Or, if you're familiar with inner work, you might feel inspired to just go to the chapters that feel most relevant to you and dive right into your personal work on these topics.

In most chapters, theoretical information is followed by examples showing you how the theory applies to what you might be experiencing in your inner and outer life, guidelines for change, and steps you can take to move out of feeling stuck. You'll most likely see some similarities in many examples to what *you* have experienced. I invite you to adapt the examples to what feels true to you.

Reading the information is the first step. In order to create changes in your life, it is important to apply the information you are reading and practise using the tools. To support you in this process you'll find a Universal Human Needs List, a Feelings List, a Tapping Protocol for Dissolving Limiting Beliefs, and a Road Map for Navigating the Trigger Response and Getting to the Gems in the back of the book. If you like, come back to certain chapters whenever you need support with specific issues in your life.

I wrote this book so you have information and guidelines on how to find and change the limiting beliefs that have made their way to you and are affecting your life. I wrote it for you to support you in moving out of limitation and coming back to wholeness and to being who you truly are. From my heart, I wish you well on your journey.

Introduction

We come into this world as perfect, innocent little beings—our souls in tiny bodies still connected to who we really are—sometimes with blissed-out little smiles when we're sleeping. What is it about us as babies that draws others in? Maybe it is not only that our bodies look cute but also that we are still connected to our eternal self—a connection that most adults have long since lost and are, in parts of themselves, longing for.

What happened? How did we get from that beautiful starting point to where we are today?

In our little bodies, we are totally dependent on the adults around us. They are our world. We learn from them and believe what they say and do. We interpret their behaviours, their moods, their ways of speaking as having meaning about us. We absorb their information, little sponges that we are at that stage, with no questioning or sorting. And as we do so, we gradually move further away from who we really are, since most of the people we are absorbing the information from are already far removed and disconnected from who they really are.

We learn and adopt beliefs about ourselves, others, and the world. Most of them are the opposite of our innermost truth. They are beliefs that limit our experiences and expressions of the magnificence of our eternal beingness.

Why is it set up like this?

I don't know. I have no explanation for it, and so far, I have not met anyone who does.

What I *do* know is that most of us are feeling a longing for our true being somewhere inside us.

We know that we suffer when we believe wrong, limiting beliefs about ourselves, others, and our world—and that many of us are on some kind of journey to dissolve our limitations.

When I was doing my counselling and psychotherapy training in the 1980s, the main approaches were talk therapy, psychoanalysis, and expressive therapies like gestalt therapy. These created awareness of our feelings, experiences, and patterns, and sometimes allowed us to let off steam from pent-up emotions, but they did not change our conditioning, our programming. They did not change our beliefs.

So much has changed since then. Not only has the technological world changed rapidly, but therapy and therapeutic approaches have as well. Influenced by quantum physics, neurobiology, neurophysiology, and spirituality, we now have tools that allow us to change our imprints, programs, and learned beliefs. Learning about the new approaches and tools deriving from these fields is what this book is about.

I invite you on a journey to discover your learned beliefs. I will show you ways to reprogram your old belief patterns so you can live more joyfully and successfully, step into your well-being, and live your dreams in this life . . .

. . . and if you like, to come back to living this life on Earth as your magnificent you.

PART I

How Beliefs Affect Your Life

If a belief does not make you happy,
it is ultimately not true.

Our beliefs affect everything.

They influence our relationships, our work, our social life and our finances. They affect our confidence and how trusting and optimistic we are in choosing our steps in life. They have an effect in how happy we are. They play a role in whether we are depressed and anxious or confident and relaxed. They shape the relationship we have with ourself, with others and the seen and unseen world.

Your life and the life of every person is influenced and formed by beliefs we have!

Our beliefs create the reality of our personal and our collective life on the planet. Their influence on our life is enormous.

Take a moment and let the next two sentences sink in a bit:

- How you live your life is based on your beliefs.
- What you believe creates the reality you experience and makes up your whole life.

What do you believe about how happy you are allowed to be? How you are allowed to be and feel when you when you are together with others? Are you allowed to fulfill and live your dreams?

Your beliefs affect every aspect of your life.

You might find yourself in similar life situations over and over again, and you might have tried to change that cycle. You might have tried different behaviours and coping strategies to shift out of old habits and repeating thoughts and feelings, and nothing much really changed. You're still finding yourself ending up in similar situations and experiences, with your same habits, thoughts, and feelings. Over and over again.

That's because you didn't change your beliefs. You can't change your life and keep your old beliefs. The beliefs will always pull you back to *their* truth! But when you find your beliefs, when you know where they came from and how you got them, then you have the choice to change them. Which will change your life.

Chapter 1

Where Do Your Beliefs Come From? How Do They Become Ingrained in You?

Has anyone ever said to you, "You just have to change your belief," without explaining exactly how to do that or how you ended up with that belief in the first place? It's easy to say, "You just have to change your belief." It's a whole other story to actually do it. The first step is to find out where your beliefs came from. That's what this chapter is about.

What is a belief?

In this book I use the term "belief" to mean thoughts that have become entrenched in your thinking and messages that ended up in your subconscious. Some of our beliefs are conscious, but most of them are subconscious. Some are supportive and others are limiting. Some are personal, but most are collective.

In this book the main focus is on **limiting beliefs**. Most limiting beliefs have their origin in trauma. The word "trauma" comes from Greek and means "wound." I use it in this book to describe woundedness at all levels of our human experience—physical, emotional, mental, sexual, energetic, and spiritual. Woundedness, which most of the time creates limiting beliefs, can be caused by large or small traumatic events, a one-time traumatic event or chronic trauma, your own personal trauma or the trauma of someone before you. Woundedness can also come from shared collective trauma.

I was born in Germany in the late 1950s and grew up in an average family of that time. My parents were busy creating a life for their little family, as most young parents do. And even though the events and actions of the war and the Holocaust were over, the memories of them were in all people. The energy of this collective trauma was everywhere, and I felt it. I thought so much of how I grew up had to do with that recent history.

I moved to the West Coast of Canada when I was thirty-one. When I started working as a counsellor, I realized my clients had had childhoods similar to mine. They had mothers and fathers who thought, felt, and behaved much like mine did. They were talked to and treated similarly to how I had been talked to and treated growing up. I was puzzled. Maybe my childhood hadn't been mainly influenced by my birth country's recent history after all.

This was the beginning of my realizing that what our parents thought and felt and how they behaved—all of which affects us as children—was way older than recent history. I realized that it's the beliefs that our parents hold that affect how we were treated growing up. Most of these beliefs were created way before our parents were born and were passed down through generations over hundreds of years.

It is limiting beliefs that cause our personal and collective traumas. And these traumas keep our limiting beliefs alive.

When we become aware of our personal and collective limiting beliefs, we can change them—and subsequently end the cycle of trauma. We can create well-being and happiness for ourselves and contribute to the well-being and happiness of others.

Where do your beliefs come from?

When you understand where your beliefs come from, you can take your first step toward diminishing the power they have over you.

Why is that?

The moment you realize your beliefs are a product of your life and other people's lives and the lives of many people before you, you understand that beliefs are made up. You understand that your beliefs are *not you*.

Let's look at **the possible sources of your beliefs:**

- Your childhood experiences.
- Your parental lineage and ancestry.
- The society, culture, and religion you grew up in.
- Past lives.

Beliefs from your childhood experiences

Everything you experienced growing up made you feel something, whether it was good, bad, or kind of neutral. When you felt good, your needs were met by the people who cared for you and provided by your environment. When you felt bad, your needs were not met. You connected thoughts to the experiences that were important to you in a positive or negative way and gave them meaning. You formed beliefs about them. When your needs were met and you felt good, you created a supportive belief. When

> *Sources of your beliefs:*
> - *your childhood experiences;*
> - *your parental lineage and ancestry;*
> - *the society, culture, and religion you grew up in;*
> - *past lives.*

you had experiences in which your needs were not met and you felt bad, you created a limiting belief.

Those experiences can be big traumatic events, but most commonly they are smaller traumatic experiences. These smaller traumatic experiences are so common and prevalent that they appear to be "normal," because almost all of us experienced them. They are the "little" emotional woundings which we experience as children in relationship with others. Often, they are not taken seriously. They are not seen as traumatic because the adults who contributed to them experienced them as well and have not healed them. Therefore, these relational traumas stay hidden in our families and societies, and are normalized. Until we become aware of them and aware of their impact on our life. Until we find the limiting beliefs we formed because of them. Until we recognize these events as trauma and heal them.

Let's look at a couple of examples of how supportive and limiting beliefs got created.

Let's say your parents really showed interest in your life and experiences. They asked you how your day went. They validated your feelings and what you needed and met your reactions to your daily happy and not-so-happy encounters with empathy. You felt really good being listened to by your parents. You felt understood, validated, respected in your choices, and supported by them.

You gave these validating experiences meaning. And that meaning turned into beliefs like:

"I am worthy."

"What I feel matters."

"What I need matters."

"My experiences and reality matter."

"I matter."

We call these beliefs **supportive beliefs**. They support us in having our needs met. They make us feel good and happy.

Now let's imagine you're back in grade school: You came home just after your mom. There were grocery bags on the kitchen floor. Your younger siblings sat in front of the TV, fighting over some candy. Your dad was still at work and your mom was stressed. The household felt chaotic. Without asking how you were or how your day was, your mom told you to unpack the grocery bags. After that you set the table. Your mom heated up some dinner. At the dinner table your brother and sister were messing around with the food. Your mom tried to stop them. She didn't pay much attention to you.

Nobody seemed interested in how your day was, what you experienced, how you were feeling. You learned not to ask for what you needed. You didn't want to burden your mom. You learned not to share much.

From repeated experiences like this, you formed beliefs like:

"My feelings and needs don't matter."

"I don't matter."

"I am a burden if I ask for what I want."

"Others don't care about my feelings and what I need."

"Others don't care about me."

We call these beliefs **limiting beliefs**. They make it hard for us to get our needs met. They make us unhappy.

Endless scenarios, situations, and experiences when we were growing up contributed to the beliefs we formed as children. The most important beliefs—our core beliefs—came from our families. They came from the interactions we had with our parents, siblings, grandparents, and maybe aunts, uncles, and cousins, and interactions we witnessed. They also came from our experiences in school. How we were treated by teachers and classmates. Being graded and compared to others. Being included in or excluded from groups. All of these experiences had a huge impact on our beliefs. They shaped what we believe about who we are, what we are able to do, and what we can have and be in our life.

Our experiences in our families and in school also contributed to our creating beliefs that determined our confidence in social interactions. In families, but even more so in schools, we got the idea that there is a "normal" that we have to measure up to. This "normal" can be about ways of learning, ways of behaving, and physical appearance—our weight, height, looks, hair, clothes. We learned to believe that if we are not "normal," there's something wrong with us. We created beliefs about what we might have to do, be, and say in order to be accepted, liked, and loved by others.

Beliefs from your parental lineage and ancestry

Let's look at a possible scenario.

Imagine your mom never really asked for what she wanted. She catered to the needs of everybody else in the family, but not to her own. Not that others demanded that from her or pressured her into it—she just chose to do it.

Your mom's behaviour was motivated by her beliefs. She might have had beliefs such as:

"I have to take care of everybody."

"A woman always cares for others first."

"In order to be loved I have to care for others."

"What I need does not count."

"My needs come last."

You might find now that you act similarly to your mom. You might find that you have a tendency to put other people's needs first, that you take care of others even if they don't ask you to.

No one told you to do that when you were growing up. Nothing traumatic or threatening happened in your childhood that caused you to put others' needs first in order to feel safe. No, you absorbed it from your mom's behaviour, from her feelings and energies, and her unspoken beliefs that were "in the air." As children, we all absorb spoken and unspoken messages from the people close to us.

If you look more closely at the beliefs that you and your mom have in common, you might realize that your grandmother had the same beliefs. Most likely your great-grandmother did too. And if you know the history of your lineage, you might strongly suspect that your great-great-grandmother had the same belief . . . and her mother . . . and her mother.

And with that you have found an ancestral belief.

Beliefs from the society, culture, and religion you grew up in

You are strongly influenced by the beliefs of the society, culture, and religion you grew up in. These beliefs are sometimes hard to recognize as beliefs, especially when your society, culture, and religion are the reality you've been in since you were born.

Such beliefs are created and kept alive by what most people in a society, culture, or religion believe and live by. There is often no clear line between these beliefs. Over time a religious belief can influence a culture so much that it turns into a cultural belief. If a society is made up of people of the same culture, this belief is then also a societal belief.

Whether we like it or not, we have societal, cultural, and religious beliefs about gender roles, childrearing, work, family values, money, social behaviour, and social, economic, and political structures. Even though some beliefs seem to be more relevant to our personal lives and others more relevant to our collective lives, our personal beliefs are deeply interconnected with our collective realities.

Let's look at some examples:

- You might find that every time you to speak to a doctor, a lawyer, a professor, the boss of your company, or a politician you feel somewhat nervous, intimidated, and unsure of yourself. Even though you do know what you want to say, something in you dreads it a bit and even tries to avoid it. You're getting tired of feeling like this, and you talk with your friends about it. You find out that they feel similarly. You become curious about what's going on. You notice that you believe that people in these roles and positions have more "power and authority" and therefore more of a say than you do. You discover an old belief that says, "You shouldn't question people in authority." You then realize that this belief is widely held in the society you live in and that it also affects the dynamics in that society's social, economic, and political structures.

- As a man, you might feel really stressed when your wife is upset with you for always working late. In return, you get upset with her for being upset. Both of you decide to figure this out. You discover that you have a belief that is shared in your culture and society: "A man needs to provide for his family" and that you draw the conclusion "The more I provide, the better husband and man I am." Your wife does not share this conclusion. She would like more help with household tasks and caring for the children and would like you home for that. She is also longing to share more emotional closeness with you. For her, meeting *those* needs would make you a better husband, and so she does not actually appreciate you for working late so often.

- Your child is unhappy in his class and with his teacher. He doesn't want to go to school. It's a struggle to get him out the door every morning. You understand that your child doesn't want to go, but you feel pressure to send him to school even though you are home all day. You don't really understand why you feel this pressure until you become aware that you have the belief, shared in your culture and society, that "children have to go to school."

Cultural, societal, and religious beliefs change over time. For example:

- In Western cultures and societies, the beliefs "A man shouldn't cry—and for sure not in public" and "A woman shouldn't show anger—and for sure not in public" are in the process of changing. Intellectually you might not believe these beliefs anymore, but you notice that you get somewhat uncomfortable when you see a man cry or a woman express her anger in public. This shows that the shift of these beliefs is not quite complete yet.

- In the West, the cultural and societal belief "Children should be seen and not heard" has completely changed over the last two generations. When a child expresses herself, you are likely to listen and to value what she has to say.

- A belief that has dominated Western cultures and societies in the last century is "You are successful if you are independent and self-sufficient." Other cultures don't hold this belief. However, people in Western societies are starting to notice a need and longing to return to a sense of greater connectedness and dependency on each other for their well-being.

- Certain religious beliefs older generations might have grown up with overlapped significantly with cultural and societal beliefs of the time. Beliefs like "Sex before marriage is wrong" or "Abortion is a sin." These beliefs changed over the last two generations, and for many people they are no longer true.

- Some religious beliefs are not as widely believed anymore. For example, "Only a priest can absolve you from your sins" or "In order to learn about God, you have to go to church." These beliefs have changed and feel outdated to many people.

What societal, cultural, and religious beliefs were true for your parents and grandparents? Which of them are not true for you anymore? And which ones are still true for you today? You might notice that some of your inherited and adopted beliefs really touch and influence you while others seem less relevant. Stay connected to the ones that touch you and explore them more closely. You can use the concepts in this book to guide you in transforming them if you like.

If you grew up with the beliefs and rules of a traditional religion or church, or a religious faith organization, the beliefs and rules you learned can have a huge impact on your life. They might affect your self-worth and your judgment of yourself and your behaviour as good or bad. You might have accepted rules that turned into beliefs about your gender role, family values, or work and income. Such rules can affect your relationship with God, the Highest Consciousness, or Source (whatever concept and word resonates most for you). They can affect your sense of who you truly are and your experience of Oneness with All-That-Is.

Depending on the groups a society is made up of, cultural and religious beliefs can be shared or vary widely among the people of that society. If a society is made up of people from the same culture and religion, their societal, cultural, and religious beliefs will significantly overlap. If a society is made up of groups of many different cultures and religions, the overlap of societal, cultural, and religious beliefs will be smaller.

Beliefs that can differ strongly between different religions and cultures often concern gender roles and behaviours—beliefs about how men and women should relate to each other, the value and worthiness of boys and girls, women and men in the different stages of their lives, and age and aging. They are beliefs about how families should live together and beliefs about the roles of community.

We often don't recognize that societal, cultural, or religious beliefs are just beliefs when we live in the society, culture, or religion that holds these beliefs. They appear to us as reality and feel like "truth."

It's much easier to recognize societal, cultural, and religious beliefs in societies, cultures, and religions other than our own —just as it's much easier to recognize both limiting and supportive beliefs in others than in ourselves.

Why is that? It is because our own beliefs feel, appear, and seem real. They feel true to us.

You might live close to neighbours who have very different cultural and religious beliefs. Knowing the history of those beliefs makes it much easier to understand the other person. It helps us to step out of our personal differences. It invites us to see the togetherness of all of us in the creation of our human story and how each one of us plays a part in it.

Beliefs from past lives

Sometimes there is no clear source from this lifetime that explains a particular limiting belief. It might also seem unlikely that this belief came from your society, culture, religion, or ancestral lineage. An unexplainable belief like this often relates to fears and phobias and can have its source in traumatic events of past lives. For example:

"I am scared of snakes."

"I am afraid of drowning when I am on a boat."

"I am scared of water."

"I am scared of heights."

"I am not safe to let my light shine."

"If I speak my truth, I'll be killed."

How did your beliefs become ingrained in you?

You have formed many beliefs through your own experiences and have been exposed to lots of beliefs from the people who came before you! Many of these beliefs are limiting beliefs about yourself, others, and the world that you formed through your own traumas. No wonder you might feel at times that you've lost your sense of who you really are. It is not your fault these limiting beliefs are ingrained in you. You are not bad, unworthy, or less because of it. It is simply part of where our human development is right now in terms of our evolution, and you are a natural part of it. In this book we focus on the awareness and healing of these traumas and the dissolving of their limiting beliefs.

Let's take a little more time to explore how beliefs from different sources have become ingrained in you.

How did you create these beliefs from your experiences? How did you end up absorbing beliefs that your parents and grandparents carried? How did messages from people close to you, and from society, culture, and religion, turn into *your beliefs?*

We find the explanation in the brainwave states we experience as children. The expression "children are like sponges" sums it up. Your main brainwave states when you are a child are different from those when you are an adult.

Here is some basic information on brainwave frequencies in different stages and activities in our life.

Brainwave states are measured by an electroencephalogram (EEG) and are distinguished by their amplitude and frequency.

As newborns and babies, our brain functions mostly in **delta brainwave** frequencies. *As adults*, these are the frequencies we are in when we are sleeping.

As toddlers, we move more into a **theta brainwave** state. When we are in theta brainwave states, information from the outside goes directly into our subconscious. *As adults*, this is the state we experience in deep meditation or hypnosis.

As young children, from about two to five years old, we are predominantly in **theta**, moving more into **alpha brainwave** frequencies with each passing year. *As adults*, we are in alpha frequencies when we are present and awake in the moment. When we focus on our breath or body sensations. When we are "in the zone" during creative activities. When we are present in the now.

In childhood, our right brain develops first where the alpha brainwaves tend to register. The right brain lets us perceive everything as one. It gives us access to intuition, play, imagination, creative expression, and the sense of connectedness to All-That-Is. When we are in theta or alpha, our inner world of imagination is as real to us as the outer world.

From around seven years on, our left brain increasingly develops, and we shift more and more from alpha into **beta brainwave** frequencies, which are more dominant in our left brain. We start to gain access to left-brain functions: logic, language, writing, reading, and linear thinking. Beta brainwave frequencies and left-brain function are the waking state of *most adults* in Western societies. In beta, we have access to alertness and to logical and critical thinking.

> *As a child in theta and alpha brainwave states, you absorb information directly into your subconscious.*

So, when you are a little child, you function primarily from your right brain in theta and alpha brainwave frequencies. In these brainwave states you absorb information directly into your subconscious. You don't have access to the discernment of logical, linear, and conceptual thinking that you have as an adult in beta and left-brain functions.

You are that "little sponge." You absorb information through feelings, your five senses, your sixth sense, and the sequences of your experiences. You feel the feelings of the people around you—you sense the energy of their thoughts. You feel the effect of their behaviour on you and the effect of your behaviour on them. You feel the effect of people's behaviour on each other. You take in information about your environment through your five senses. You sense the atmosphere in places, and energies in and between people with your sixth sense.

And because you don't have a discerning beta brainwave state available to you yet, you can't question the messages you get from others. You believe not only the stories of Santa Claus, the Easter bunny, and the tooth fairy to be real and true, but just as readily you believe messages such as "You are so stupid," "You are too little," "You are fat," "You can't do that," "That is bad," and "You are bad." You don't have the brain function yet to ask yourself or others, "Is that really true?"

When you are in theta and alpha frequencies and right-brain function, you live in a reality of "all is one." When you are in those brain functioning states as a child, your outer and inner worlds are not clearly distinguished. You feel part of everything around you. You are part of a field of information, and you can feel and sense all that's there. You relate to everything in this field. There is nothing you are separate from. That means everything that you experience and witness has something to do with you. You interpret the behaviour and feelings of others as *having meaning about you.*

When others around you were unhappy, it meant something about you. Maybe you started to think you were not good enough because you couldn't make them feel better.

And when you were laughed at, criticized, or ignored, when your feelings and needs were not noticed, when you were hit, abandoned, yelled at, grounded, or excluded—all these smaller and bigger traumas, that you experienced with the people around you—it influenced the beliefs you formed about your worthiness, lovability, safety, and capabilities.

Endless scenarios and others' behaviours have influenced your beliefs about your relationship with yourself, others, and your place in the world.

Some of your interpretations of your experiences were *misinterpretations*. You could only understand what you experienced from your limited life experience and from the theta and alpha brainwave state you were in. For example, when your parents were unable to understand and validate your feelings and needs, you might have interpreted it as "My feelings and needs are not important," while in truth your parents were traumatized themselves, and emotionally not skilled enough to tune into your feelings and needs and validate them.

If you experienced bigger traumas and were physically, emotionally, or sexually abused, you likely formed the belief "I am not safe." And this was true for you growing up. You therefore formed beliefs about safety, about what you had to do and how you had to be in order to feel safer. For example:

"When I don't move and when I am really quiet, I am safe."

"If I don't say what I think, I am safe."

"I have to make others feel better so that I am safe."

"If I don't say what I need, I am safe."

When you are a child in alpha and theta brainwave states and your outer and inner realities are equally valid and not clearly distinguished, the outer world and others have the power to determine your inner world. When you are a child, your immediate family and caregivers *are* your world, and you have no other world to compare it to.

When we are growing up, most of us don't have adults there for us especially in the more subtle traumatic experiences, who accept us and validate what we feel and sense. We have nobody who puts our experiences into a wider context and greater perspective for us. Therefore, we create beliefs out of what we feel, sense, see, and hear by interpreting our experiences from our limited understanding as a 3-, 4-, 5-, 6-, 7- . . . year-old. These beliefs get stored in our subconscious and usually stay unconscious and unexamined.

Until, that is, later in life, when we notice that we are somehow blocked in aspects of our life. When we create experiences and life situations we don't like. Or we hear or read about beliefs and learn to examine our own.

Once we start examining our beliefs, what we discover are those beliefs of our 3-, 4-, 5-, 6-, 7- . . . year-old selves. We become aware that we have been running our lives based on the meaning that the little child we were was able to give their experiences and on the messages they were given.

> *Once we start examining our beliefs, we become aware that we have been running our lives based on the meaning we made as a little child and the messages we were given.*

No matter whether a belief affects your life a little bit or immensely, the principles behind how these beliefs became ingrained in you are the same. No matter whether the beliefs stem from personal, ancestral, societal, cultural, or religious sources, they end up as beliefs programmed into your subconscious.

And even though we are focused here on the creation and forming of *limiting* beliefs, the principles of how you formed and ended up with your *supportive* beliefs are the same.

Our limiting personal beliefs are shared collectively

What does that mean?

It means that the beliefs that feel so very personal to us are actually shared by many other people. Many of these beliefs stem from widely spread traumas that are seen as "normal" and have gone through many generations. And so, we have often the same limiting beliefs or variations of them. Here are examples of the most common ones:

"I am not good enough."

"I am not worthy."

"I am not lovable."

"I am bad."

"I don't belong."

"I don't deserve . . ."

"I don't matter."

"There is something wrong with me."

"I am less than others."

"I am not wanted."

"I can't."

"Life is hard, life is a struggle, life is not fair."

"I can't have what I really want."

"I can't trust."

"I am all alone."

We often judge ourselves as "bad" or "less" for having such beliefs. We might be embarrassed about them. We might feel shame about the traumas we experienced that are at the bottom of these liming beliefs. This can make sharing both, the traumas and these beliefs, challenging.

I have often experienced that when people start to share their beliefs and their smaller and larger traumas, and hear others do the same, they find out how similar their traumatic experiences and beliefs are. They realize they are not alone in this and feel a huge sense of relief.

When we share our beliefs, we realize that they are a product of our upbringing, our societies, cultures, and religions. We understand that we are all in this together. That we experience this collectively. None of us is alone in our limiting beliefs. When we examine them, we can see more clearly how made-up—often formed by traumas—and untrue these limiting beliefs really are.

Let's take a belief that many people have in common, the prevalent limiting belief in our Western culture: "I am not good enough." This belief can show up as variations like:

"I am not good enough, therefore nobody wants to be with me."

"If someone is unhappy, it means I am not good enough, because I couldn't make them happy."

"The way I am is just not good enough."

"If I am good enough, I will be accepted, liked, loved."

"I have to do . . . in order to be good enough" (e.g., "If I take on extra chores, then I might be good enough").

"I have to be . . . in order to be good enough" (e.g., "When I am more spiritual/more educated/more helpful/kinder/slimmer, then I will be good enough").

"I have to have . . . in order to be good enough" (e.g., "When I get that next degree/promotion/job/house, then I will be good enough").

The variations are endless.

In summary, a belief like "I am not good enough" could come from a variety of sources and experiences, including:

- making meaning out of your experiences when you were little,
- being labelled, criticized, belittled, mocked, or put down by your parents, siblings, peers, and teachers,
- comparisons made in school and families,
- your parents and their parents and their parents who carried that belief themselves,
- messages that were collectively shared in your society, your culture, and your religion in the time of your upbringing, and
- past lives.

The truth is, being worthy and good enough is innate to each one of us. Your worthiness and good-enoughness *cannot* be determined by anything or anyone. You are worthy and good enough—and you always have been.

We might know a truth like this intellectually—and we *do* know it in our heart and soul—but that does not change our subconscious programming and how we *feel* about it.

Chapter 2

The Repeating Cycle:
Your Experiences Create Your Beliefs
Your Beliefs Create Your Experiences

You might notice that you have unfulfilling, similar, and repeating experiences in your relationships, your work, your finances, your happiness level. You're aware that you often find yourself in similar feeling states and thought patterns, many of which you might not really like.

You might have even changed partners, changed jobs, or moved to somewhere new in order to change these experiences, and yet you still ended up in similar situations, similar states of feeling, and similar thought patterns.

Why is that?

Growing up, you created beliefs by giving meaning to your experiences, feelings, and body sensations through your thoughts. You also took on and inherited beliefs from people before you who gave meaning to *their* experiences.

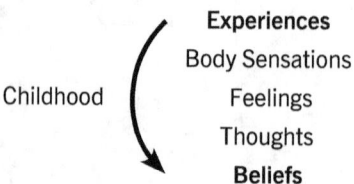

Your **Experiences** Created Your **Beliefs**

The beliefs you formed growing up create experiences later in your life. These experiences are similar to the original experiences that formed the beliefs in childhood.

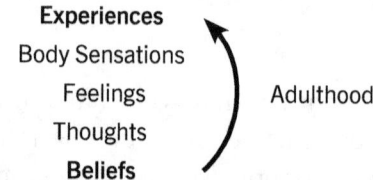

Your **Beliefs** Create Your **Experiences**

. . . and you end up in a cycle.

Let's go through this together by looking at two examples of challenging scenarios and experiences in childhood—smaller traumas that are often seen as "normal" in our society—and how they created limiting beliefs. In each example we'll fast-forward into adulthood to see how these beliefs create similar experiences to those in childhood.

Childhood experience: Let's imagine you were in elementary school and the teacher asked a question. You raised your hand and were very excited because you thought you knew the answer. The teacher called your name, but when you gave your answer, the other kids started to laugh. You had no idea why they were laughing. It didn't feel good, and the teacher didn't step in. She just asked the next child for their answer.

Body sensations

You felt a tightness in your chest, you blushed, and your hands started to sweat.

Feelings

You felt vulnerable, exposed, embarrassed, and ashamed.

Thoughts

You thought, "This does not feel good to me. I don't like to be laughed at."

Beliefs

You gave the experience these meanings: "Others don't like what I say," "When I'm excited and myself, others laugh at me," "I'm not safe in a group," or "I'm not safe being myself with others."

Adulthood experience: Now you are grown up. You are in a group setting, and everyone is talking about a topic you are excited about. You are very knowledgeable about the subject, but somehow you feel insecure and unsure about saying what you know out loud. You fear others might laugh at you when you share what you know and are excited about. You notice you feel anxious and uncomfortable when you have to speak. Your feelings are driven by the beliefs you formed back in elementary school. Beliefs that had been programmed into your subconscious.

Beliefs

You might believe: "Others don't like what I say," "When I am excited and myself, others laugh at me," "I'm not safe in a group," or "I am not safe being myself with others."

Thoughts

You might think: "I don't like speaking in groups," "Others don't like what I say," or "Others judge me."

Feelings

You feel vulnerable and exposed, and you experience a sense of embarrassment.

Body sensations

You feel a tightness in your chest. You notice that you are blushing and your hands are getting sweaty.

Experience

You have recreated your elementary school experience. You feel those old feelings and body sensations. You judge yourself and fear others will too.

Your adult experience is driven by those old beliefs.

Your **Beliefs** Recreated the **Old Experience**

Childhood experience: Let's imagine you grew up in a family where your parents' or siblings' needs were, or seemed to be, more important than yours. Maybe:

- your mother was depressed and preoccupied with her own struggles,
- your sibling(s) had something going on that meant they needed a lot of care and attention,

- your parents believed that adults' needs were more important than children's, or
- your parents didn't have the emotional ability to tune into your feelings and needs or the communication skills to talk about them.

Your experience was that others didn't pay much attention to how you felt or didn't seem to care about your needs.

Body sensations

You felt a tightness in your belly and started to build tension in your neck and shoulders.

Feelings

You felt a sense of loneliness and sadness. Maybe you felt upset and angry.

Thoughts and beliefs

You might have had **thoughts** that turned into **beliefs** like: "Others don't care about me," "Others don't care about how I feel," "I am not important," "What I need does not matter," or "I don't matter."

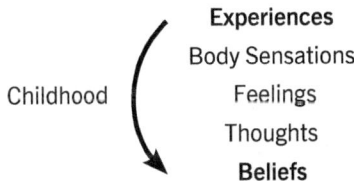

Your **Experiences** Created Your **Beliefs**

Adulthood experience: Now you are an adult, and you are in a relationship. The beliefs you formed when you were a child recreate variations of your childhood experiences.

You might not ask for what you need. Unconsciously you expect your partner to read your mind or guess your needs. And he is not very good at that.

You might communicate your needs to your partner in ways that don't invite him to give you what you need.

For example, you might say, "Why am I always the one who does the dishes?" instead of saying, "When you take a turn at doing the dishes I feel so supported and cared for by you." (See more about this in chapter 17, How to Ask for What You Want from Abundance Instead of Scarcity.)

When you say, "Why am I always the one who does the dishes?" your partner gets defensive and doesn't take a turn—and you feel stuck doing the dishes.

Body sensations

You notice tightness in your belly and tension in your neck and shoulders.

Feelings

You feel that old sadness and loneliness, and maybe you feel upset and angry.

Thoughts

You might think: "He does not care about me" or "He does not care about what I need."

Beliefs

Your old beliefs of "What I need does not matter," "I am not important," and "I don't matter" are alive in you again.

You are in a cycle: your experiences created your beliefs and your beliefs create your experiences.

CHAPTER 2 | THE REPEATING CYCLE

We *all* do this over and over again!

Chapter 3

Reactions to a Limiting Belief

There are two main reactions to a limiting belief we can experience. One is giving in to the belief. The other is trying to prove the belief wrong. Usually we are unconscious of these reactions. You are most likely familiar with both of them.

Let's explore these reactions to the very common belief of "I am not good enough."

Giving in to the belief

If you give in to the limiting belief "I am not good enough," you probably have some, or even most, of the following inner experiences:

- You feel sad and depressed, hopeless, defeated, and discouraged.
- You feel that your energy has plummeted or that your vibrancy and vitality are low.
- You give up trying to improve your life and give in to living your life in a limited way.
- You feel like a victim.

Trying to prove the belief wrong

With this reaction you're trying hard to prove to yourself and others that the belief is not true. This is *not* a conscious act. Trying to prove the limiting belief "I am not good enough" wrong might show up as working extra hard, doing many jobs, and studying more than necessary. You might even choose a career you hope will prove that you are "good enough."

The energy of all this doing feels tense. It feels like a struggle—striving and working hard without really feeling joyful. The energy can also feel pushy and too much. Somehow over the top.

When you try to prove this belief wrong, you might perform especially well at work, becoming the person who goes the extra mile. But you are not doing it for the joy of it—instead, you are unconsciously motivated by the hope that if you do your job really well, it might prove that you are good enough.

And when you achieve something that you were striving for, or others acknowledge and praise you, you might have that sense of *"See—I am good enough"* for a little while. But that sense of being good enough and the relief that comes with it is usually short-lived. Soon the subconscious limiting belief will come back to the forefront and challenge your sense of self all over again.

Have you ever tried to tell someone they are beautiful when they think they are ugly? Or convince someone of their talent when they believe they are untalented? It just does not work. The same is true for your limiting beliefs. Your behaviour of striving and hearing from others that you did your job well *cannot* change your limiting belief if it is entrenched in your subconscious programming. Your outer actions and the confirmations from others do not communicate with your subconscious belief programs and therefore are not the right approaches to changing your limiting beliefs.

The diagram below illustrates the most common feelings, sensations, and experiences of **giving in to the belief** versus **trying to prove the belief wrong.**

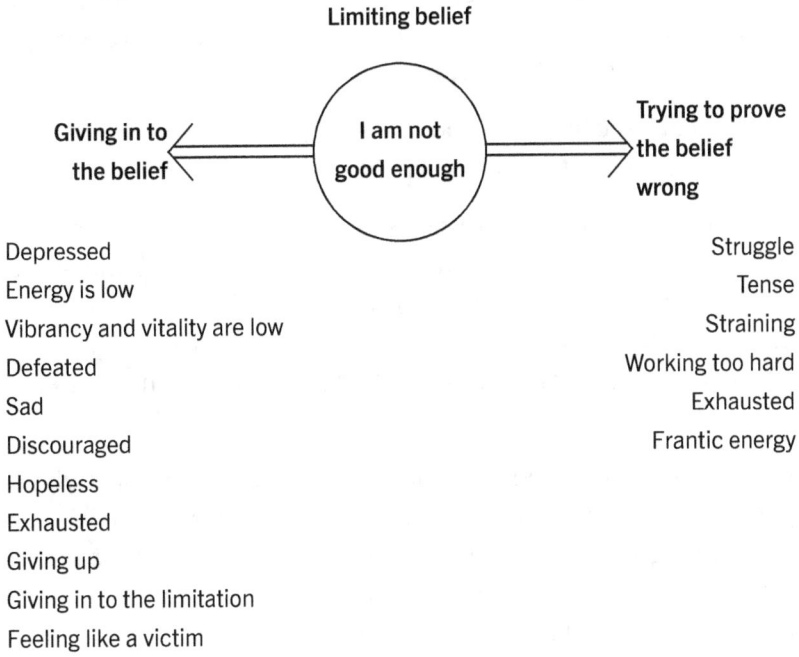

Depressed
Energy is low
Vibrancy and vitality are low
Defeated
Sad
Discouraged
Hopeless
Exhausted
Giving up
Giving in to the limitation
Feeling like a victim

Struggle
Tense
Straining
Working too hard
Exhausted
Frantic energy

Both behaviours, giving in to the belief and collapsing and trying to prove the belief wrong and straining, make people witnessing the behaviours feel uncomfortable. Somehow the false limiting belief "is in the room." Everyone except the person with the limiting belief can sense it. And since the belief is "flawed," the behaviours deriving from it feel "flawed" as well. The person's actions or words don't feel true, don't flow, don't come from joy or authentic expression, and others sense a disconnect.

When you are with a person who is giving in to a limiting belief, as an observer you get a sense of that person being a victim of their own belief and in their own life.

When you are with someone who is trying to prove a limiting believe wrong, you might experience the following:

- you feel somewhat uncomfortable without knowing why,
- you have the uneasy feeling that the other person is demanding/wanting something from you, whether it be your energy, your attention, or your approval, or
- you feel used by the other person's unconscious agenda to prove their limiting belief wrong.

We have all been on both sides of this experience—trying to prove a limiting belief wrong ourselves or being around someone who is trying to prove their limiting belief wrong. Without changing anything else, you can choose to hold yourself and the other person in compassion. By doing so, you will have already stepped out of limitation.

What is your preferred reaction? You might be someone who is pushing against their limiting beliefs. Or maybe you know yourself more as giving in to them. You might also recognize others who have a tendency to try to prove their limiting beliefs wrong and some who feel more like a victim of them.

Or, without being entrenched in either behaviour, you can shift from the trying-to-prove-the-limiting-belief-wrong reaction to the giving-in-to-the-limiting-belief reaction in a single situation.

For example, let's say you have the belief "Others don't support me." You've had a busy day and friends are coming for dinner. You ask your partner for help with the dinner preparations. Some part of you doesn't trust you will be supported. Your energy feels frantic, a bit too pushy and strained. Part of you wants to prove the limiting belief "Others don't support me" wrong, and you "push" to receive support. Your partner reacts to the *energy* of your asking and is resistant to supporting you freely. You are upset. You feel sad, defeated, discouraged, and exhausted. In this moment you see the reaction of your partner as confirmation that your belief "Others don't support me" is true. Part of you collapsed. You gave in to your limiting belief. You did not choose these behaviours and feelings consciously. They were created and driven by your subconscious belief program.

Stepping out of these two reactions

To end the repeated experience of either reaction you need to dissolve the limiting belief itself. While the limiting belief is still in your subconscious programming you will keep repeating your experiences of either reaction. Any coping strategies for trying to make these reactions feel better or changing them on the surface will not work in the long term.

You want to be really clear about the false limiting belief and dissolve it. When the limiting belief is replaced by a supportive belief, both reactional behaviours will fall away without any effort on your part.

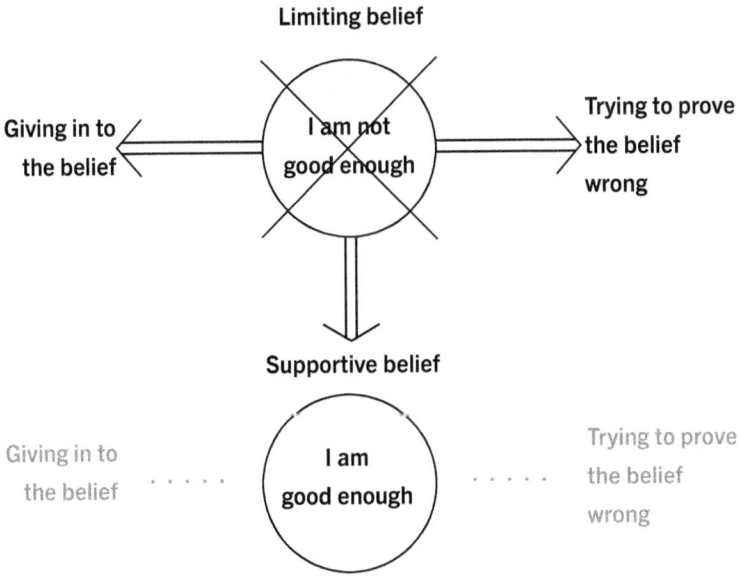

Chapter 4

Models of Limiting and Supportive Beliefs

Your actions and behaviours in your life are motivated by your needs and inspired by your goals and dreams. These are influenced by the traumas of your own and your ancestors' past and the beliefs which derived from these traumas. Here we want specifically look at the beliefs about your needs, goals and dreams for your life. How the experience of your actions and behaviours *feels* to you is influenced by the beliefs you hold about your needs, goals, and dreams.

When you hold beliefs that support the fulfillment of your needs, goals, and dreams, the experience and journey of that fulfillment is pleasant and joyful. When you hold beliefs that limit you and cause you to doubt the fulfillment of your needs, goals, and dreams, you struggle. It does not matter whether the needs, goals, and dreams are small or huge. The same principle applies.

> *It is my understanding that most anxieties and depressions stem from the effects of our limiting beliefs!*

When you hold *limiting* beliefs about the needs, goals, and dreams you are trying to fulfill, you experience feeling states of *anxiety or depression*. Both are very prevalent in our Western societies.

And with that I don't mean necessarily severe anxieties and depression that you would need to be hospitalized for. Rather I mean all the smaller and bigger moods that we all know in their different variations and shades. Feeling nervous and restless, stirred up and uncentered, worried and unsure, being tired and having low energy, feeling grumpy and lethargic, feeling disconnected and without love for your life.

It is my understanding that most anxieties and depressions stem from the effects of our limiting beliefs! I have seen countless times that the moment someone dissolves a limiting belief, the anxiety or depression they were feeling just a moment before—and had felt for years—was gone.

Let's look at this in some examples and diagrams.

You can use the diagrams to help you identify anxiety and/or depression you might experience in your life and find the limiting beliefs connected to it.

(You will notice that these diagrams overlap somewhat with the diagrams in the previous chapters. These ones look at limiting and supportive beliefs from a slightly different perspective.)

Example 1: Let's say you have a financial goal. Maybe you want financial security, or you dream about buying something in particular. You start thinking about ways to create more income. You save some money, and you are very excited about it.

Then, somewhere on your journey toward this goal, your excitement plummets. You are working so hard at trying to achieve your goal that it feels like a struggle. You notice how tense you feel. And every time you accumulate a bit more money, another, bigger bill comes in and you are right back where you started. Your struggle mixes with some anxiety, and you notice some negative thoughts building up around the idea of having more money.

What happened?

As you started to move closer toward your goal, your limiting beliefs were activated. Limiting beliefs that might make you think thoughts like:

"I don't deserve that income."

"I feel selfish focusing on having that much money."

"My friends will not like me anymore if I have more money."

"My family might say, 'Who do you think you are? You think you're better than us?'"

These beliefs pull you unconsciously in the opposite direction from where you consciously want to go. Your old limiting beliefs pull you in one direction and your goals and dreams in the other. Being pulled in two different directions is creating your inner experience of struggle, anxiety, and tension.

Let's look at this in the diagram below.

Pursuing Needs, Goals, and Dreams When Having Limiting Beliefs

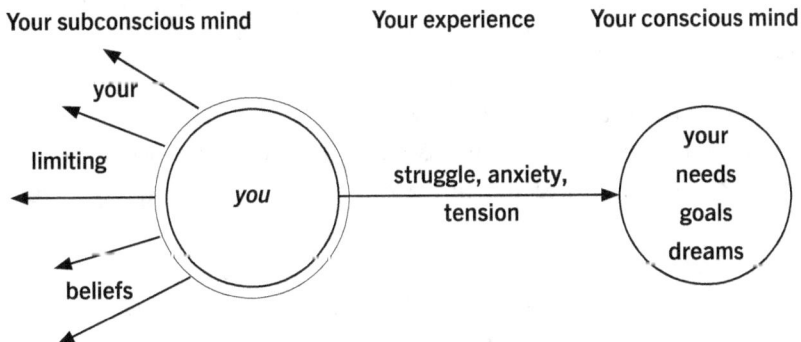

So, you **struggle** along for a while. Feeling **anxiety and tension**, and maybe even fear sometimes, as you work toward your goal. You shift back and forth, moving closer to and then further away from your goal, **doubting** yourself and your ability to achieve it. You work very hard, but there is no real flow or sense of ease. And every experience of something not working, any setbacks you face, you use to confirm that you can't reach your goal, can't live your dream. You are unconsciously confirming your limiting beliefs. You are sabotaging yourself.

What's happening in these moments?

The closer you move toward fulfilling your needs, reaching your goals, and living your dreams, the stronger you feel the tension between where you want to go and the pull of your limiting beliefs. The voices of your limiting beliefs get louder and louder and you start listening to them (again)—consciously or unconsciously.

As you get tired of this struggle, tired of feeling this tension and anxiety, you might decide to let go of your needs, goals, and dreams. You give up. And at first that might feel good. The tension is gone. The anxiety is gone. The struggle is gone. *Phew!* Those forces are no longer pulling you in opposite directions and that feels like a big relief.

But . . . as time passes, you're not feeling so great anymore.

What's going on?

You start feeling a low, collapsed energy inside you. You notice feelings of sadness and **depression**. You feel unmotivated and not excited about life anymore. You feel hopeless and defeated.

Why is that?

You just let go of the struggle. Shouldn't you be able to enjoy life now? Why can't you? When you let go of the struggle, you also let go of fulfilling your needs. You stopped reaching for your goals and following your dreams. Giving up your needs, goals, and dreams creates sadness, depression, low energy, and lack of excitement about life.

We are part of an ever-expanding universe. The life energy, that aliveness in us, always wants to move toward expansion, expression, growth, and evolution. The moment you stop the flow of life energy in you, you start feeling depressed.

Example 2: Let's imagine you have become aware that you focus a lot on making sure others around you are happy, that you often don't say how you are feeling and what you are needing. You decide to pay attention to when the old pattern shows up and to choose a different behaviour. You are motivated to place more focus on yourself and to be authentic with others. But whenever you bring your focus to your own feelings and needs, and you think about expressing them honestly to your partner and friends, you notice that your low-level anxiety (that is kind of always there) gets really intensified. It almost feels to you as if you would be doing something wrong if you shared your feelings and asked for what you need. You might even feel somewhat guilty for not behaving in accordance with the "rules" of your beliefs. And when your anxiety gets so strong that it affects you physically, you pull away from your partner and friends and spend more time on your own. At first that feels good. The anxiety has lessened. It's a relief. But after a while you notice you feel a bit depressed, less alive, and your energy feels kind of flat and low.

You experience the cycle of these feelings and behaviour often and you become curious about it. You explore more deeply what's going on inside you. In this process of exploration, you find limiting beliefs you learned growing up.

They might sound like:

"My inner reality does not matter."

"The feelings and needs of others are more important than mine."

"I should not express my feelings."

"If I say what I need, I am being selfish."

"I have to take care of the feelings and needs of others."

"It's not safe to be myself with others."

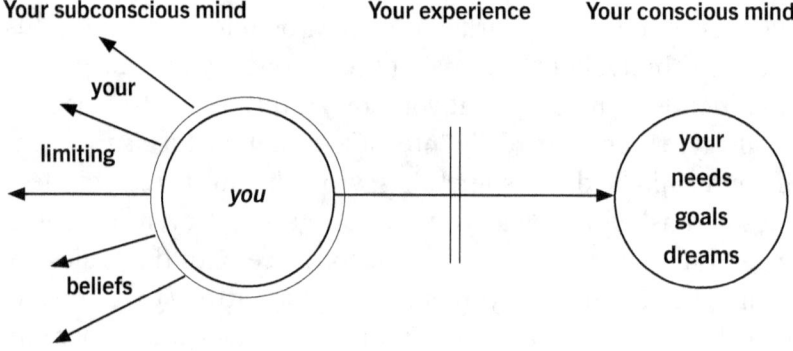

Giving Up Your Needs, Goals, and Dreams

You feel:
sad, depressed, hopeless,
defeated, collapsed, and low in energy

Letting go of the struggle seems like a good idea, but letting go of your needs, dreams, and goals is not.

Wouldn't it be good to find a better way of letting go of the anxiety and struggle?

The **anxiety**, struggle, and tension are created by the two opposite forces pulling on you. Letting go of one pulling force—your needs, your goals, and your dreams—ends the anxiety, struggle, and tension, but creates **depression.** What would happen if you let go of the other pulling force—your limiting beliefs?

When you dissolve your limiting beliefs, the anxiety disappears. And so do the tension and struggle, because you are not being pulled in two opposite directions anymore. And because you are also keeping your goals, your dreams, and your wish to have your needs fulfilled, you allow yourself to expand, and that feels inspiring, exciting, and joyful. Your sense of direction, aliveness, and self-expression is back.

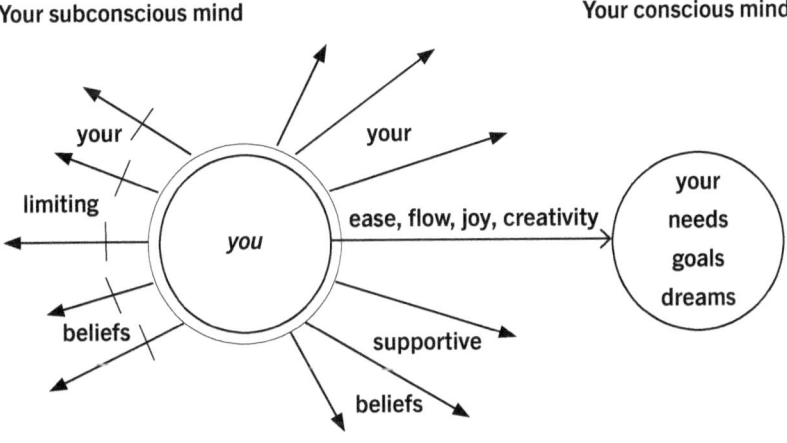

**Fulfilling Your Needs, Goals, and Dreams
When Your Limiting Beliefs Are Dissolved**

Your supportive beliefs from your conscious and subconscious programming support you in the fulfillment of your needs, goals, and dreams by pulling in the same direction as your focus and your actions. With less or no pull away from your goals, moving toward them turns into experiences of flow, joy, and fulfillment. And when something is not working, you don't use that to confirm those old limiting beliefs anymore. Instead, you listen to your supportive beliefs, which helps you to find solutions for overcoming setbacks more easily.

Chapter 5

Feelings, Needs, and Strategies

In Western societies there is little clarity about the connection between our feelings and needs, and little distinction between our needs and the strategies we use to fulfill our needs. When you understand how your feelings are connected to your needs, and when you know that you have a need versus a strategy in mind, your emotional life will become easier. It will also improve communication in your relationships!

You might find it helpful to have a look at the lists of needs and feelings in Appendix 1 and Appendix 2.

Feelings

Collectively, we have divided feelings into two categories. Those we label "negative," "unpleasant," and "bad," and those we label "positive," "pleasant," and "good."

All living beings are evolutionarily wired to seek out life-affirming conditions and avoid hindrances. So it is not surprising that people share an impulse to want to feel and try to hold onto the pleasant feelings and to avoid the unpleasant ones, pushing them away. As humans, we have collectively developed many behaviours that distract us and distance us from "bad" feelings—addictions of many different kinds, for example, can serve that purpose.

When you were growing up, you might have learned to suppress or ignore your feelings in general or you might have learned to suppress and ignore just some of them. Maybe you are aware of that now as an adult. You might be working on not suppressing your feelings anymore. You might be searching for ways not to be overwhelmed by your feelings, ways to cope with them better. You might have found ways to communicate your feelings. You might have more compassion for yourself and others in terms of the feelings you and they experience.

To become aware of how you feel and to be accepting, kind, and gentle with yourself in all of your feelings is really important.

Needs

When you look at the list of needs, you can see that we have a wide range of needs—from physical and connection needs, to needs for self-expression. Our needs are universal. We all have the same needs. A need is general. It does not say anything about how we fulfill it.

Strategies

We call the specific ways in which we fulfill our needs "strategies." We often confuse strategies with needs. We might say, "I need you to turn down the music." And because we use the word "need" in our statement, we might *think* it is our need. What we are actually communicating is *a strategy for having our need fulfilled.*

Here is a guideline you can use to find out whether you are dealing with a strategy or a need: When you think of **a person, an action, a time,** and **a place** to fulfill your need, you have a strategy in mind!

Chapter 5 | Feelings, Needs, and Strategies

One need can be fulfilled by very different strategies. And one strategy can fulfill many different needs.

Strategies to fulfill a specific need vary from person to person and change over time—the season, the time of day, week, and month—and with the culture, subculture, and the family we live in.

Let's look at some examples of strategies in the context of one of our human core needs: connection.

Here are different strategies for how people fulfill the need for connection:

- A woman gets together with her girlfriends to fulfill her need for connection.
- Someone else might regularly meditate and experience a deep connection to Self and All-That-Is.
- Another person likes to go to football games with thousands of people cheering for their team and feel connected to the people in the stadium.
- A child asks to be held by his parents to feel connection.

Each strategy is different from the others, but they all fulfill the same need: the need for connection!

What are your preferred strategies to fulfill your need for connection?

One Need Can Be Fulfilled by Very Different Strategies

Which strategies do you prefer to fulfill a need you have? If you like, select a need from the needs list and write down the strategies you usually use to fulfill that need. Then imagine you could find new strategies to fulfill it. What would they be? Then take one of these strategies you found and see what other needs it fulfills.

Just as one need can be fulfilled by many different strategies, one strategy can also fulfill many different needs.

Many Different Needs Can Be Fulfilled by One Strategy

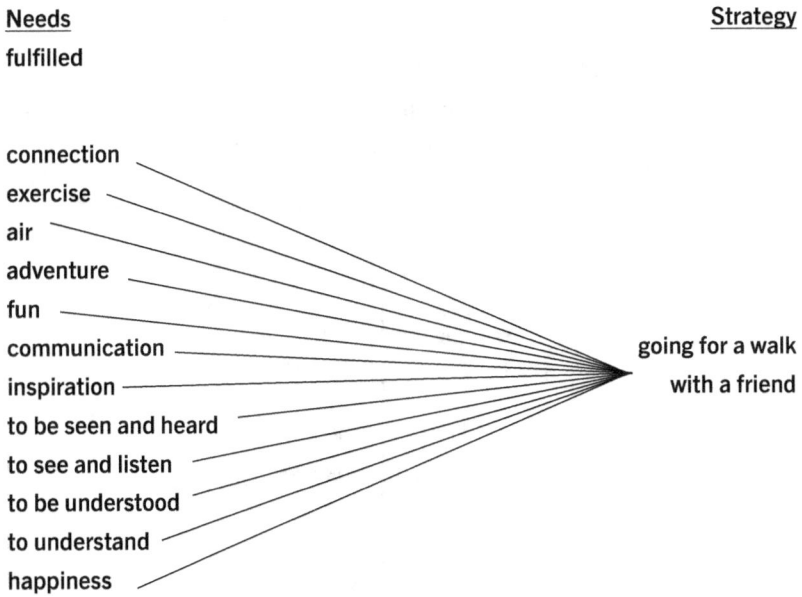

How feelings and needs are connected

Many of us are preoccupied with our feelings. We can get caught in a cycle of spending a lot of time and energy on them. Maybe you notice that you judge yourself for having unpleasant, "bad" feelings. You might think you are making progress when you have "good" feelings. You might suppress some of your feelings and express others more freely. Maybe you have learned coping strategies for feelings you experience as challenging. Perhaps you struggle to communicate your feelings, or you might be very open about expressing them. **You are in a cycle of focusing on your feelings.**

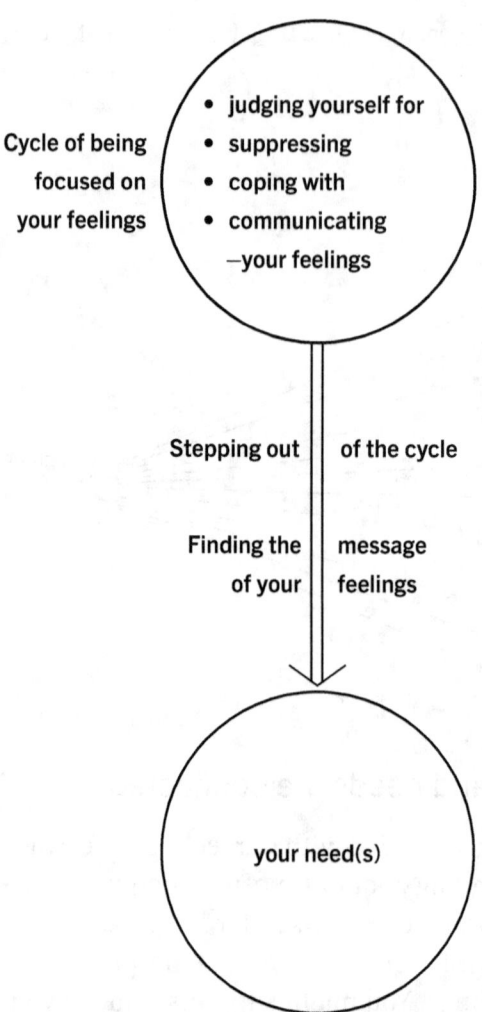

I invite you to step out of the cycle of being focused on the feelings and instead look at your feelings as messengers and signals of your needs.

I invite you to acknowledge and accept *all* of your feelings and become curious about how they can give you information about whether or not your needs have been met. There is no feeling that is disconnected from your needs.

CHAPTER 5 | FEELINGS, NEEDS, AND STRATEGIES

Here is a very true and simple guideline to remember:

When you have a pleasant feeling, it means your need or needs have been met.

When you have an unpleasant feeling, it means your need or needs have *not* been met.[1]

Let's look at an example.

You notice that you are feeling somewhat sad, kind of pulled in. You start to be curious about why you feel that way. You think about your new job and your colleagues and that you really like them. You realize you've felt sad and a bit pulled in since this morning when you heard them talk about how much fun it was to meet for a drink last night at this new place. They hadn't asked if you wanted to join them.

You recognize you have a need to be included. And you make the connection between how you feel (sad and pulled in) and your unfulfilled need (inclusion).

> *When you have a pleasant feeling, it means your need or needs have been met.*
> *When you have an unpleasant feeling, it means your need or needs have **not** been met.*

When you notice a need, take a moment to acknowledge it and allow yourself to have that need. When you do this, the feeling—in this example, sadness—shifts.

The moment you listen to the feeling (sadness) and you find the underlying need (inclusion), the feeling has served its purpose as a messenger. When you listen to the message your feeling has about your needs, the job of the feeling is done. You don't

---

[1] The concept of the connection of feelings and needs was taught extensively by Marshall Rosenberg in his teachings and writings about nonviolent communication (NVC). See Marshall B. Rosenberg, *Nonviolent Communication: A Language of Life* (Puddle Dancer Press, 2003).

have to work so hard at coping with your feelings anymore. The sadness in this example might drop away and you might notice gentleness, a sense of calm and compassion for yourself instead.

Or you might notice that you are feeling angry now because this need for inclusion has often not been met. You realize it started when your older brother and sister did not include you in their games. Your feeling (anger) is the message of your unmet need (inclusion), in this case your need in the more distant past.

You might have experienced that sometimes the unpleasant feeling shifts only for a little while and then comes back even though you found the underlying need. When that happens, you most likely have a limiting belief about this need that is keeping the unpleasant feeling present. (See more about this in chapter 7, Beliefs about Your Feelings and Needs.)

The more you value your feelings as communicators and messengers of your needs, the less important it becomes to figure out how to cope with them. You don't need to be concerned anymore about having "bad" or "good" feelings. They *all* are just messengers of your needs. Judging your feelings as good or bad will drop away. And instead of focusing on expressing your feelings, you check inside yourself first to examine what needs are being met or not met. You have stepped out of the feeling cycle.

Sometimes you might notice that you have needs that conflict with each other. You might feel physically tired and you are also excited by the thought of going out with your friends. You have a need for rest and sleep and also for fun and adventure. See if you have a pattern in how you navigate your conflicting needs. You might realize that you override your need for rest often and go out with your friends instead. Or maybe you often say no to invitations because you are tired, even though part of you has a need for fun and adventure. When you are aware that your needs are conflicting, you have a chance of finding strategies that can fulfill both of them in ways that feel good to you. For example, you could rest first and meet up with your friends later, or you could go out with your friends but go home early to get a good sleep.

The more you create a habit of connecting your feelings with your needs, the easier it will get.

The needs and feelings lists in Appendix 1 and Appendix 2 are helpful for this process. You could make a few notes about them and keep them in different places in your house, your car, your bag, or at work.

If you like, take a moment right now and remember a happy moment from today. Find the feeling that you felt and your need that was fulfilled. Use the lists of needs and feelings to help you. Allow yourself to really acknowledge the need or needs that were fulfilled today and feel the gratitude you have for all that contributed to that fulfillment. The moment you do that, you create a deeper connection with yourself and others, and a greater love for the experience of your own life.

Our feelings, needs, and strategies in relationship with others

Remember, your feelings let you know whether your needs are being met or not met. When you have happy, pleasant feelings, those feelings are telling you that your needs are fulfilled and met. When you have unhappy, unpleasant feelings, those feelings are letting you know that your needs are unfulfilled and not met.

We often project our feelings onto other people. When we project our unhappy, unpleasant feelings onto others, we can become angry at those people. We become upset, impatient, or frustrated with them or even blame them for our own unhappiness.

When we project our happy, pleasant feelings onto others, we like them and love them. We might adore, praise, and admire them.

Actually, most of our feelings toward others have very little to do with the other person. Instead, our feelings have a lot to do with our own needs. The other person just happens to be either contributing to the fulfillment of our needs or hindering it.

Let's look at this in a very basic example: Let's say your need is for connection. It's evening, and you'd really like to have someone to be with and talk to. Your partner is not home yet. You get upset and angry at your partner for working so much and so late. But then your friend phones, and you have a lovely, long conversation. You feel heard, you listen, you share, and you feel connected to your friend. The phone call ends. You are feeling good, your heart is open, and you are feeling happy. Your partner is still not home, but you notice that you are no longer upset or angry at him. In fact, you actually feel this warmth and love toward him.

> *Most of our feelings toward others have very little to do with the other person. Instead, our feelings have a lot to do with our own needs. The other person just happens to be either contributing to the fulfillment of our needs or hindering it.*

What happened?

The feelings of upset and anger that you had toward your partner were showing you your unfulfilled need for connection. That need was fulfilled by the phone call with your friend. You then felt good and happy, and your heart felt open. These were messages that your need for connection was fulfilled.

First you projected your unhappy feelings—anger and upset—onto your partner. Later you projected your pleasant feelings—warmth and love—onto him. Your partner did not change in that time! He was not even present. All of these feelings, thoughts, and needs happened within yourself. Your partner was the person you projected your feelings and needs onto.

It's almost easier to see when the other person is not present.

The strongest realization of this for me was during a season of tree planting. It was my first summer in Canada. I spent some weeks in the majestic wilderness of the Coast Mountains in British Columbia, bags with tiny little trees that needed to be planted hanging from both sides of my body. Climbing up those steep slopes and planting those little trees in rough terrain in the sun, rain, snow, heat, and cold was the hardest and most challenging work I have done in my life. It pushed my boundaries physically, emotionally, energetically, and spiritually. I was by myself in the wilderness, with the trees and my shovel, and all my experiences, feelings, and needs. There was no one there I could project anything onto. I realized every feeling I was feeling and every need I noticed were my own. No one was responsible for them but me.

The moment you project your feelings and needs onto another person, you give them power over your feelings and needs. You make the other person and their behaviour responsible for how you feel. With that, you give away your choice of your feelings and the fulfillment of your needs. Owning your feelings and needs can be very empowering.

When you are aware of your feelings and are able to connect them to your needs, it is also easier to give yourself empathy. Doing that, you hold yourself in unconditional compassion in the feelings and needs you are experiencing. Here are words you could use to express empathy with yourself:

"It makes so much sense that I feel confused and upset. I need more transparency and clarity."

"No wonder I feel sad. I need some comfort because… happened."

You can do the very same for another person, giving empathy by understanding their feelings and needs without judging them or their experience.

But often we are not free of judgment. Often our struggles with others are caused by their needs and strategies conflicting with ours. Just as we label feelings, we label strategies as good and bad, right and wrong, and we are often convinced that our strategy, our way, is the right one. Collectively, we have patterns of judging others for their strategies. Often our disagreements, arguments, and the fights we have with each other are about our differences in strategies.

What we don't realize is that these are just strategies we are fighting about—not our needs! But when we are not clear about what is a strategy and what is a need and we think they are the same somehow, we feel threatened; we feel that if we accepted a different strategy, our needs would not be met. In some sense we are afraid that if we give up the strategy we have in mind, we might have to give up the possibility of fulfilling our needs.

When we know the difference between a need and a strategy, it is easier to step out of conflicts like these and become curious about the need(s) we are trying to fulfill. We have more flexibility and freedom in choosing our strategies. We can see that we don't need to fight about and defend one strategy. The moment we find our need and can see the other person's need, something shifts.

In that moment we might notice these changes:

- We sense a connection with the other person that we didn't feel just a moment before.

- We are free to realize that the fulfillment of our needs is not actually threatened by the other person or their need(s).

- We can relate to the other person's need and see their strategy in a different light.

Chapter 5 | Feelings, Needs, and Strategies

- We can choose to stay with our need(s) and let go of the strategies we were fighting about.
- We can choose new strategies, knowing there are many to choose from.
- We can find strategies that fulfill both our needs and the other person's needs.

When you see your feelings as messengers of your needs and when you know that as humans we all have the same needs and that you can choose from many different strategies to fulfill your needs, you will sense an inner freedom and more ease in your relationships.

Chapter 6

How Do You Find Your Beliefs?

When you don't know your limiting beliefs, they influence your life experiences without your being aware of it. Time alone neither changes your limiting beliefs nor heals the trauma that caused them. In order to be empowered to consciously influence your life, you need to become aware of your limiting beliefs. Then you have the choice of changing them.

"How am I going to find these limiting beliefs if most of them are subconscious?" you might wonder.

Since most of your beliefs are subconscious, you need to listen to and look at the *messages that come from the subconscious* to find them. This is easier than you might think.

Let's look at how to do it.

> *If what you are feeling, sensing, thinking, and experiencing makes you happy, it is driven by a supportive belief. When your needs are fulfilled and you live your goals and dreams, that fulfillment is co-created by your supportive beliefs.*
>
> *If what you are thinking, feeling, sensing, and experiencing in your life makes you **unhappy**, it is driven by a limiting belief. When your needs are unfulfilled and you are **not** living your goals and dreams, that nonfulfillment is co-created by your limiting beliefs.*

Remember:

- Your experiences when you were growing up created your feelings, body sensations, and thoughts and formed your beliefs. These beliefs now create similar thoughts, feelings, body sensations, and experiences in your adult life.
- The fulfillment or nonfulfillment of your needs is influenced by your beliefs.
- The choices you make about your actions and non-actions are based on your beliefs.
- The fulfillment or nonfulfillment of your dreams and goals in all areas of your life is supported or hindered by your beliefs.

This knowledge is what you use to find your limiting beliefs. You are listening to and looking at the messages from your subconscious when:

- you pay attention to your feelings, your body sensations, and your thoughts,
- you pay attention to the fulfillment or nonfulfillment of your needs,
- you become aware of your behaviours and your actions, and
- you look at the areas of your life in which you are living your goals and dreams and the areas in which you are not.

These messages direct you to your beliefs!

If what you are feeling, sensing, thinking, and experiencing makes you happy, it is driven by a supportive belief. When your needs are fulfilled and you live your goals and dreams, that fulfillment is co-created by your supportive beliefs.

If what you are thinking, feeling, sensing, and experiencing in your life makes you *un*happy, it is driven by a limiting belief.

CHAPTER 6 | HOW DO YOU FIND YOUR BELIEFS?

When your needs are *unfulfilled* and you are *not* living your goals and dreams, that nonfulfillment is co-created by your limiting beliefs.

Often, we don't like to look closely at what makes us unhappy and not feel good. Some part of us knows it has to do with old painful situations, experiences, and traumas of the past. These painful old situations and experiences are connected to our limiting beliefs. It can feel scary and daunting to go there. But when the pain of not living fully gets louder in you and you get tired of repeating experiences that make you unhappy, something in you might be ready to revisit the old experiences that created your limiting beliefs.

This book contains tools to help you navigate the memories of old painful, challenging experiences and unsettling feelings of traumas. The main tool in this book, Emotional Freedom Technique, also called tapping, is a powerful tool that enables you to navigate overwhelming and strong emotions. When you tap, part of you holds yourself and your memories and feelings in gentleness, kindness, and acceptance. It's almost as if there is a part of you that acts like a loving parent who is present and caring for the younger you in all their painful experiences. And yes, you will feel old strong feelings and remember old painful situations in this process of discovering and dissolving your limiting beliefs. When you tap, you will feel these feelings and remember old situations—but only for a short time. Then they will lose their power and start to shift. The more you practise the more you learn to trust that these old painful situations and feelings no longer hold power over you. With every round of tapping they shift. (See Part II for more information on tapping.)

When you feel ready and you want to find your limiting beliefs, use the list of questions below to increase your awareness. It will support your listening to the messages of your subconscious.

Choose the questions you feel drawn to:

"What am I feeling?"

"What am I sensing in my body?"

"What am I thinking?"

"Which of my needs are fulfilled?"

"Which of my needs are not fulfilled?"

"In which areas of my life do I live my dreams?"

"In which areas of my life do I not live my dreams?"

"How do I behave in certain situations?"

"What actions do I take?"

"What actions do I not take?"

To relate your answers of these questions to your beliefs, ask yourself, "What must I believe . . . "

"that I feel this?"

"that I sense this in my body?"

"that I think this?"

"that these needs of mine are fulfilled?"

"that these needs of mine are unfulfilled?"

"that I behave like this?"

"that I take these actions?"

"that I don't take these actions?"

"that I live my dreams in this area of my life?"

"that I don't live my dreams in this area of my life?"

Chapter 6 | How Do You Find Your Beliefs?

You want to be really present with what you are sensing and feeling in your body. It is helpful to adapt a gentle and accepting attitude to the information that your body sensations, your feelings, your memories, and your thoughts are giving you. You might also notice images or sense energies. All of these are messages from your subconscious about your beliefs and the traumas that created them. They are your allies in finding and identifying your old learned and inherited beliefs.

What you find will be either supportive beliefs or unsupportive beliefs.

In this book we are focusing on how to find **unsupportive, limiting** beliefs.

Here are examples of limiting beliefs that many people have. Several might resonate with you.

"I am not good enough."

"There is something wrong with me."

"I am not lovable."

"I am not allowed to ask for what I need."

"I am too much. My feeling, needs, experiences are too much."

"I am a burden."

"I am too sensitive."

"I am not safe with others."

"The feelings and needs of others are more important than mine."

"I am all alone."

"Nobody is there for me."

"I don't need anybody."

"I am not allowed to be happy because my parents were not happy."

"I can't be happy because I am not good enough."

"I am only loveable if I take care of other people's needs."

"I have to be perfect so others want to be with me."

"If I make a mistake, I am not safe."

"If I focus on my own feelings and needs, it means that I am selfish."

"If I have lots of money, my family will think I am better than they are."

To get to what your limiting beliefs exactly sound and look like, you can use different statements and try them out. You might notice you can actually *feel* whether they are right for you or not. When you find the right words and the right statement for your limiting belief, something will "click" for you. And you'll know: "That's it!"

Here are some phrases you can try out and use for your belief statements:

"I am . . ."

"I am not . . ."

"I can't . . . because I . . ."

"I can't . . . because others . . ."

"I can't . . . because of . . . [situation]"

"I can only . . . if I . . ."

"I can only . . . if others . . ."

"I can only . . . if the situation . . ."

"If I reach my goal, then I will be . . ."

"If I reach my goal, then others will be . . . "

"If I do . . . that means that I am . . . "

"If I have . . . that means that I am . . . "

"If I am . . . that means that I am . . . "

Let's go through this process of listening to the messages of your subconscious to find your limiting belief with the following examples.

Each example shows a starting point, questions you can ask, and the underlying limiting belief(s). Each example has a different starting point. The starting point is what is first in your awareness. The other messages will show up if they are important. Each starting point is equally valid. Any one of them can lead you to your limiting belief.

Starting point: Feelings and body sensations

Experience
Feelings
Body sensations
Thoughts
Beliefs

You are aware that you often feel anxious **(feeling)** in meetings, and you start paying attention to what else you might notice.

You find that you are sensing tension and a constriction in your throat **(body sensation)**.

You notice that you are thinking that everyone else in the meeting has more to say than you do (thoughts).

And you ask yourself these questions:

"What do I believe that makes me feel anxious?"

"What do I believe that causes my throat to close up?"

"What do I believe that makes me think everyone else in this meeting has more to say than I do?"

Then, like puzzle pieces coming together, you become aware of these old beliefs:

"I am stupid." (This belief gets really activated when you are in meetings.)

"Others criticize me."

"Others judge me."

"Others laugh at me."

"I am less than others."

"I am not safe." (In meetings)

Maybe you remember situations from school where you were laughed at when you spoke. Or times at the dinner table with your family when you were criticized and judged. Through memories like these you can find your experiences that contributed to forming your limiting beliefs.

No wonder you feel anxious!

The anxiety, tension, and constriction in your throat, and your thoughts that you are less than everyone else—all of these are created by those old beliefs. And those beliefs recreate your experiences in meetings over and over again.

Starting point: Thoughts

Experience
Feelings
Body sensations
Thoughts
Beliefs

You might notice repeating **thoughts** that have been there for some time. For example, you might continuously have a thought such as, "I can't have a partner because I am too big/too thin/too tall/too short/too uneducated/too educated/too rich/too poor/not attractive enough . . . "

Without having to explore your feelings or body sensations, you can ask yourself, "What do I believe that makes me think this?" You might find that the thought "I can't have a partner because I am too big" *is* already a belief. You might want to be curious about what else you believe is connected to this.

And underneath this specific belief you might find a more general belief:

"I am not good enough to have a partner."

"I don't deserve a partner."

"I am not wanted."

"I am not lovable."

Starting point: Behaviour

Behaviour
Beliefs

You notice that you say "I'm sorry" a lot. Especially after you say what you really think and feel. After you are quite open and direct. Others wonder why you apologize so often.

You get more and more annoyed with this **behaviour** of yours, and you become curious about what's behind it.

So you ask yourself this question: "What do I believe that makes me say 'I'm sorry' so often?"

You remember situations from growing up and you realize that you learned to believe thoughts about yourself like these:

"When I am myself, others don't like me."

"When I am myself, I am too much for others."

"When I am myself, others don't want to be with me."

"When I am myself, I am a burden."

Starting point: Non-actions

Non-actions
Beliefs

For years you have had a job that you don't really like, but every time an opportunity for a new job comes up:

- You don't make the phone call.
- You don't write the email.
- You don't fill out the application.
- You miss the deadline.

The opportunity passes, and you are still in your job that you kind of hate!

You ask yourself: "What must I believe that I don't take action to change my job?" You realize that your mom and dad were in jobs they didn't like for their whole lives. You remember them coming home after work, complaining about their jobs. And from their messages you learned beliefs like these:

"You can't have what you want in life."

"Work sucks and you just have to get through it."

"You can't do what you like and love and make a living."

"Life is a struggle."

"Only fortunate people have good jobs. I am not one of them."

Starting point: Needs

Needs
Feelings
Body sensations
Thoughts
Beliefs

You become aware that you often feel disrespected by others. Your **need** for respect is not being met. You have experiences such as being put down, dismissed, or made the subject of condescending remarks.

Your feelings might be sadness or anger.

Your body sensations might be a tightness in your chest or a knot in your belly.

You ask yourself these questions:

"What must I believe that others don't respect me?"

"What must I believe that causes my need for respect not to be met?"

Then you listen to what comes up and you might find that you believe:

"I don't deserve to be respected."

"I am less than others."

"I am not as worthy as others."

Starting point: Dreams for your life

Dreams for Your Life
Beliefs

You look at the areas of your life that feel really good and the ones that don't. You realize that you have a generally happy relationship and really good friends, but money is always tight. You're tired of not being sure if you can pay your bills every month. You are ready to make some changes.

And you ask yourself this question: "What must I believe that I never have quite enough money?"

You might find that you learned to believe ideas about money like:

"People with money are not happy."

"I can't have everything."

"I am a people person—I am just not good with money."

"If I had lots of money, my friends would not like me anymore."

You also find that you have positive, supportive beliefs about relationships:

"I am worthy of a good relationship."

"I am lovable."

And you have positive, supportive beliefs about friendships:

"Others really like me."

"Others want to be with me, and I want to be with them."

"It is safe to be close with others."

The fulfillment of each area of your life is supported or limited by your beliefs.

This means that:

- the areas of your life in which you live your dreams are co-created by your supportive beliefs, and
- the areas of your life in which you don't live your dreams are co-created—restricted—by your limiting beliefs.

So, when you are unhappy with an area of your life—work, relationship, friendships, social life, finances, fitness, the shining of your soul in your life—you can ask yourself this: "What must I believe that makes me experience this?"

Starting point: Getting triggered

Another powerful way to find your beliefs is to become aware of your inner experiences when you are triggered.

When you are triggered, your feelings, body sensations, and thoughts are all activated in an accelerated and charged experience.

Because it is fairly complex to find your limiting beliefs through your trigger experience, there is more information and a step-by-step process for it in chapter 9, Getting Triggered.

In summary

In order to find your beliefs, you don't have to examine, analyze, and figure out your whole life history—you can go from any starting point and find the connection to your belief-programming.

You might notice that you have a tendency to be more aware of your thoughts than your feelings. Or more aware of your body sensations than your thoughts. Or you are really conscious of some stuck and repeating behaviour and not so much of your feelings. Go with what you are aware of. That is a beautiful starting point.

Chapter 7

Beliefs about Your Feelings and Needs

Your beliefs about your feelings and needs have an immense influence on how you relate to yourself and others. Because of their crucial impact on your emotional well-being, we'll dedicate this whole chapter to them. It also revisits some of the information you will already be familiar with from reading chapter 6, How Do You Find Your Beliefs?

Just like your beliefs about everything else, beliefs about your feelings and needs are either supportive or limiting.

How are your limiting beliefs about your feelings and needs formed?

Limiting beliefs about your feelings and needs are created by:

- your personal experiences growing up and the meaning you gave them,
- what your parents believed and modelled,
- your experiences at school and in social groups,
- generally held beliefs in the society and culture you grew up in, and
- rules you were taught through your religious tradition.

Limiting beliefs about your feelings created by your personal experiences growing up and the meaning you gave them

You might have been shamed, put down, sent away, ignored, or laughed at when you showed sadness, fear, anger, upset, or excitement as a child.

You might have been told:

"Don't be sad."

"Anger is not getting you what you want."

"There is nothing to be afraid of."

"Get over it."

"Don't get so excited. You'll make yourself sick."

Or there might have been a general uncomfortable silence when you expressed how you felt.

Out of these messages and experiences, you formed limiting beliefs about your feelings like:

"When I am sad, there is no one there for me."

"I am bad if I show anger."

"I shouldn't feel scared."

"It's not safe to show that I am scared."

"I shouldn't be so excited."

Limiting beliefs about your feelings created by what your parents believed and modelled

Maybe your mom never really expressed anger. She got sad instead. She pulled back into herself. Your dad, on the other hand, often got angry. He never said he was afraid. He didn't show sadness often. Your parents thought that being polite with friends and neighbours meant never expressing their true feelings.

From witnessing your parents' behaviour, you might have adopted your mom's way of suppressing anger and getting sad instead. You learned to pull back inside yourself. Or you might have a tendency to get angry easily, when you are actually afraid or sad. You might stay on a polite conversational level with neighbours and friends. You don't express your real feelings with them.

From witnessing your parents' behaviour and sensing their beliefs, you formed your own beliefs about your feelings:

"As a woman, I should not get angry."

"It's not manly to feel and show that I am afraid."

"It's not polite to show my feelings with neighbours and friends."

Perhaps you experienced a parent expressing their feeling, possibly anger or sadness, in a way that was harmful to others in the family. So you formed the belief "Feeling or expressing anger or sadness hurts others." You vowed to yourself to never feel or express those feelings.

Limiting beliefs about your feelings created by your experiences at school and in social groups

At school you showed your feelings of being upset, angry, anxious, sad, or frustrated with schoolwork or situations you were in with other kids, but you were not met with understanding and empathy from the teacher and/or your classmates. Maybe you were even sent into the hallway or to the principal.

You might have heard messages like:

"There is no reason to be upset about this."

"You are making it extra hard with your frustration."

"Anger is not going to help you."

"You are such a crybaby."

Through these messages and experiences you learned not to express your feelings at school anymore. After some years you even stopped paying attention to how you were feeling at school. Later, at college, university, or even at work, you notice that you often feel some unease or anxiety.

From your experiences at school you might have formed beliefs that looked and sounded like:

"I am not safe to feel and express my feelings with others."

"Others don't like me when I am upset."

"Others put me down when I am sad."

Limiting beliefs about your feelings created by generally held beliefs in the society and culture you grew up in

When you were growing up, there might have been generally held beliefs in your society and culture like:

"Men don't cry."

"Showing your feelings is being weak."

"You don't show your feelings in public."

"Women shouldn't be angry."

Limiting beliefs about your feelings created by rules you were taught by your religious tradition

You might have received messages like:

"You should not feel jealous."

"To be impatient is bad."

"You should not feel resentful."

"God sees all your bad feelings."

How to find your beliefs about your feelings

We all learned beliefs about:

- which feelings are good or bad,
- which feelings we are allowed to have and express, and which ones we aren't,
- what it means about us and others when we feel or express a certain feeling, and
- what will happen when we express a certain feeling.

These beliefs keep us from easily accepting each one of our feelings and from seeing them plainly as messengers for our needs and using them as guidance for our life.

You can find your beliefs about your feelings by looking at the experiences you had growing up.

Here are some questions that will help you find these beliefs:

- Which feelings were okay and not okay to *feel* in your family when you were growing up?
- Which feelings were okay and not okay to *express* in your family when you were growing up?
- Were there different rules for adults and for children?
- How did these rules differ for men (your dad), for women (your mom), and for boys and girls in your family?
- How did your parents, siblings, friends, schoolmates, and teachers respond when you expressed your feelings?

If you were to *feel* a feeling now that you had learned to label as bad or not okay:

- What do you think would happen?
- What would feeling this feeling mean about you?

If you were to *express* a feeling now that you had learned to label as bad or not okay:

- What do you think would happen?
- What would expressing this feeling mean about you?

Here are some general beliefs about feelings. Which ones resonate with you?

"My feelings don't matter."
"My feelings do matter."

"My feelings are not important."
"My feelings are important."

"Others don't care about my feelings."
"Others do care about my feelings."

"It is not safe to show or express my feelings."
"It is safe to show or express my feelings."

"If I show or express my feelings, I am weak, bad, stupid, wrong . . . "
"If I show or express my feelings, I am empowered, strong, clear, alive . . . "

"If I show or express my feelings, others will laugh at me/ridicule me/get angry at me/put me down/criticize me/ignore me/hurt me . . . "
"If I show or express my feelings, others will listen to me/validate me/support me/like me/be there for me . . . "

You might also have formed some beliefs about the feelings of others in relation to yourself. Here are some examples of what they might sound and look like:

"I am responsible for the feelings of others."

"If someone is angry, it means I did something wrong."

"If someone is unhappy, I have to make them feel better."

"If someone is unhappy, it means I failed and I am not good enough."

Here are some beliefs about specific feelings. Which ones resonate with you?

"**It is not okay to feel** sad/angry/scared/upset/very happy/excited/confused/ frustrated."

"**It is okay to feel** sad/angry/scared/upset/very happy/excited/confused/frustrated."

"**It is not safe to show that I am** sad/angry/scared/upset/very happy/excited/confused/frustrated."

"**It is safe to show that I am** sad/angry/scared/upset/very happy/excited/confused/frustrated."

"**When I show or express that I am** sad/angry/scared/upset/very happy/excited/confused/frustrated, others will laugh at me/ridicule me/get angry at me/put me down/criticize me/ignore me/hurt me/not want to be with me."

"**When I show or express that I am** sad/angry/scared/upset/very happy/excited/confused/frustrated, others will listen to me/validate me/support me/like me/be there for me."

"**When I show or express that I am** sad/angry/scared/upset/very happy/excited/confused/frustrated, it means that I am weak/bad/stupid/wrong."

"**When I show or express that I am** sad/angry/scared/upset/very happy/excited/confused/frustrated, it means that I am empowered/strong/clear/alive."

Your beliefs about your needs

How your beliefs about your needs were created is very similar to how the beliefs about your feelings were created. You can apply what you read about your feelings to your needs.

How do you find your beliefs about your needs?

You can find your beliefs about your needs by looking at your experiences when you were growing up and how they related to your needs.

Here are two questions to help you find these beliefs. They are similar to the ones about your feelings:

- Which needs were okay to have in your family?
- Which needs were not okay to have in your family?

Here are some needs to start with:

- connection, love, and affection
- safety and trust
- nurturing and comfort
- empathy, consideration, and support
- inclusion, equality, harmony, and peace

Chapter 7 | Beliefs about Your Feelings and Needs

- learning and competence
- independence, spontaneity, and creativity

Use the needs list in Appendix 1 to find more of your needs.

- When you were growing up, were there different rules for which needs were okay to express for adults and children? Men, women, boys, and girls?
- What were the responses from your parents, siblings, other family members, friends, teachers, and schoolmates when you voiced or expressed your needs?

Here are some general beliefs about needs. Which ones resonate with you?

"My needs don't matter."
"My needs do matter."

"My needs are not important."
"My needs are important."

"Others don't care about what I need."
"Others do care about what I need."

"It is not safe to express my needs."
"It is safe to express my needs."

"I have to fulfill other people's needs first before I can fulfill my own needs."
"I can freely choose to attend to my needs first. I can freely choose to attend to the needs of others.

"If I express my needs, others criticize me/ridicule me/put me down."
"If I express my needs, others listen to me/support me/take me seriously."

Here are some sentences you can use to find your beliefs about specific needs. Complete them by looking at the list of needs and selecting the ones that fit your experience. For example: "It is okay to ask for *food*. It is not okay to ask for *comfort*."

"It is okay to ask for . . . "
"It is not okay to ask for . . . "

"It is safe to ask for . . . "
"It is not safe to ask for . . . "

"When I ask for . . . it means that I am needy/not capable/selfish."
"When I ask for . . . it means that I am confident/trusting/loved."

"When I ask for . . . others will criticize me/ridicule me/put me down."
"When I ask for . . . others will help me/support me/be there for me."

When you go through the list of needs, you might find needs that you didn't even know existed. Those are needs that were simply not part of your experience growing up in your family.

When you find your beliefs

When you find your limiting beliefs about your needs you can see that these needs were not met very well for you when you were growing up. Now, as an adult, most likely you find that it's still hard to get these needs met. These needs feel like a big deal in your life.

You also know that some other needs in your life are more easily met. You most likely had them fulfilled while you were growing up and you formed supportive beliefs about them. In your adult life they are met for you most of the time, and when they are not, you don't really get upset about it. These needs are not a big deal in your life.

Chapter 7 | Beliefs about Your Feelings and Needs

What you think and feel, and how you behave in your relationships and in social situations, has to do with your beliefs—and often these beliefs are about your feelings and needs. You might find that knowing these beliefs helps you understand yourself better in your thoughts and feelings, reactions and behaviours in your relationships with others.

Some of the beliefs you found will feel good and make you happy; others will not. Knowing your beliefs gives you the choice and power to change the limiting beliefs about your feelings and needs into supportive beliefs. These supportive beliefs will help you create more fulfilling and happy experiences in your life.

When you have dissolved limiting beliefs about your feelings and needs, you will be able to:

- experience more ease and freedom to be authentically you in your relationships and in social situations,
- feel and express your feelings and needs in ways that feel good to everyone around you,
- have your needs met more easily, and
- be more authentically present for the feelings and needs of others.

> **Remember, beliefs are only learned, and what has been learned can be unlearned.**

Chapter 8

Our Beliefs Form Our Reality

If a belief does not make you happy, it is ultimately not true!

You might be thinking, "Are you kidding? What I believe *is* true. My life proves it. What do you mean it's not true?"

What you believe can feel very true because it appears to be the reality in your personal life. It might also look like the reality in your culture or society, but ultimately it is made up. It is a created and agreed-upon reality.

What I mean is, if a belief does not make you happy, it is not true in your heart and in your soul.

Let's look at that a bit more closely.

There are three aspects of yourself that judge the truth of your beliefs differently.

- **Your heart and soul:** There is always a part of you that knows which beliefs are true and which are not. Let's call this part your unconditioned heart and soul. It is the place that little children speak their truth from—sometimes shockingly to the "conditioned" adults around them. Your heart-and-soul-knowing has never forgotten that you are lovable, worthy, and one with everything.

- **Your intellect**: Besides your heart-and-soul-knowing, there is also what you believe intellectually. This is often aligned with your heart-and-soul-knowing. In other words, your intellect knows that you are as worthy as everyone else. But sometimes your intellect differs from your heart and soul in the assessment of your beliefs because it is influenced by the collective agreements, rules, and beliefs of the society and culture you live in.

- **Your conditioned self/your subconscious programming**: And then there is the conditioned and programmed part of you that learned and inherited supportive and limiting beliefs about yourself, others, and the world. This part of you believes your learned and inherited beliefs to be true. Both your supportive and your limiting beliefs.

So, each one of these aspects of yourself might hold a different belief!

Here is a general guideline:

- **Your heart and soul** do not hold limiting beliefs.
- **Your intellect** holds both supportive and limiting beliefs, and sometimes knows that your learned limiting beliefs are not true.
- **Your conditioned/programmed you** holds supportive and limiting beliefs and does not question them.

Your reality is mostly influenced by your subconscious programmed beliefs!

At times you might be amazed or even shocked at how different your subconscious beliefs are from what you intellectually believe to be true. Your beliefs are actually more aligned with what you experienced, saw, and witnessed as a child growing up than with what you now think intellectually as an adult. This shows up especially in the beliefs about your sense of self, relationships, gender roles, and money.

A few years ago, I took a closer look at my money beliefs because despite my excellent training and the really good work I did, my income was low. When I started to tap on my money beliefs, I was surprised to find that I was holding and living by the money beliefs of my parents from the time when I was growing up. Beliefs like:

"Women don't need much money."

"A woman is supported financially by a man."

"A woman should not earn more than a man does."

I was shocked. I did not believe these beliefs intellectually. But when I cleared those beliefs, my income dramatically improved without me working on any major changes in my work and career!

> *There are three aspects of yourself that judge the truth of your beliefs differently:*
>
> **Your heart and soul** *do not hold limiting beliefs.*
>
> **Your intellect** *holds both supportive and limiting beliefs, and sometimes knows that your learned limiting beliefs are not true.*
>
> **Your conditioned/programmed you** *holds supportive and limiting beliefs and does not question them.*

A belief can really look like reality. This applies to our personal beliefs as well as our collective beliefs.

You might hold beliefs like "I am not good enough" or "Life is a struggle." And these beliefs show up as experiences in your life. You often feel you are not good enough, and every time something is difficult, you experience life as a struggle. It feels like a confirmation of your beliefs.

These beliefs also create a certain filter through which you perceive your reality. You will have a tendency to interpret outer situations and inner experiences according to your beliefs. You see and notice more readily what is familiar to you and what you believe. You're more likely to overlook experiences that do not confirm your beliefs. This selective perception confirms to you the "truth" of your limiting and your supportive beliefs.

If you hold the belief "I am not good enough," you will more readily notice situations where you failed at something and overlook and not count the situations where you did things well. You might also be very self-critical and have very high expectations of yourself, ready to find every little flaw and sign of not-being-good-enough.

Our collective beliefs are collectively made up and agreed on. They are created throughout our evolutionary process and modified over time.

Our dominant collective beliefs are based in duality: higher and lower, better and lesser, good and bad, worthy and unworthy. We apply them to things, experiences, people, animals, and plants. We experience the effects of these beliefs in our personal lives, and we act out these beliefs globally.

Currently, in most human societies, we have a collective belief of "We need money in our lives." It is such an agreed-on reality that it is hard to see a belief underlying it. Imagine working without the concept and use of money. What if that were possible?

At different times, different cultures held the collective belief "The Earth is flat." People were afraid of the edge of the Earth. They were afraid of the unknown beyond that edge. They were afraid they might fall off if they reached it.

That belief might make you smile or shake your head now, but it was so real for people back then. It was their reality. We can see that beliefs change over time.

It always seems easier to recognize the personal supportive and limiting beliefs of others than to notice our own. And it always seems easier to see the collective supportive and limiting beliefs of other times and cultures than to be aware of the collective beliefs of the time and culture we live in.

You can use this knowledge to get more clarity on your limiting beliefs. You could ask yourself:

"What would my children/grandchildren say about this belief I have?"

"What would a person from another culture say about this belief I have?"

Since our personal and collective beliefs and realities are made up, you can choose to "unmake" them. You can choose to create something different.

You can ask yourself:

"Does this belief make me happy?"

"Does this belief make my heart and my soul happy?"

Then use the "dissolving limiting belief process" (see Part II for more on this) for your limiting beliefs and let the beliefs that are true in your heart and soul come back to you. They will help you create a life you will thrive in.

Here are beliefs that might make your heart and soul sing:

"I am always worthy, like everyone else."

"I am always good enough, like everyone else."

"I am always lovable, like everyone else."

"I am one with everything."

**The beliefs that are true in your heart
and soul will make you happy!**

Chapter 9

Getting Triggered

Being triggered can be a powerful way to find your limiting beliefs. When you're triggered, your feelings, body sensations, and thoughts are all activated in a speeded-up and highly charged experience. When you become aware of what exactly is going on inside you during your trigger experience, you have an amazing opportunity to find your limiting beliefs! Because when you are triggered, most of the time it's because an old limiting belief has been activated in you.

Navigating a trigger response is challenging. To be able to do it well, it helps to have information about what is going on inside you. It takes practice to shift from an automatic reaction to choosing how you want to respond instead.

Let's walk through this step by step.

What does "getting triggered" mean?

You might be familiar with the term "getting triggered." It means something old was woken up inside you or in someone else who got triggered. In this book I use this term to mean when something emotionally uncomfortable, upsetting, or scary is activated and we perceive another person or a situation as a threat.

Being triggered takes us out of the present moment. We react to something from the past.

Triggers mostly come from information we perceive through our five senses. Something that we see, hear, taste, touch, or smell can awaken memories of an experience that was threatening to us in the past. The information can also come through our sixth sense, when we sense an atmosphere or a certain energy. Most of the time we get triggered by something another person says or does.

So, when we get triggered, we experience something in our surroundings that awakens the memory of an experience that was threatening to us in the past. Most triggers for those of us in Western cultures are perceived as emotional threats. If you experienced physical or sexual trauma in the past, your triggers can be sensed as physical or sexual danger.

The physiological responses to getting triggered

Let's look at what happens in your brain and body when you get triggered.

When you perceive something as dangerous, parts of your brain get activated and set the fight, flight, or freeze response into motion.

This happens through hormonal, chemical, and nerve communications between different parts of your brain, the glands of your body, and your autonomic nervous system. Your autonomic nervous system gets activated and your adrenal glands release stress hormones (adrenaline, noradrenaline, and cortisol). In the fight or flight response, the activation of the sympathetic branch of your autonomic nervous system is dominant. In the freeze response, it's the parasympathetic branch. Your organs, muscles, and senses get activated and your body is ready to fight, flee, or freeze to keep you safe.

Whether you are in real danger and really need to fight, flee, or freeze, or you are in a situation that is not actually dangerous but that you perceive as dangerous, the responses in your brain and body are the same.

Your emotional experiences when you are triggered

When you are triggered, a part of your midbrain, the limbic system, registers something as dangerous. The amygdalae are part of this limbic system. These almond-shaped structures sit in both sides of your midbrain and are commonly known as the amygdala. The amygdala plays a central role in "detecting danger" and starting the fight, flight, or freeze response.

Your prefrontal cortex, the part of your neocortex that sits behind your forehead, and the amygdala have communication pathways between them via neural and neurochemical connections. Most of the time your prefrontal cortex is in charge, signalling to the amygdala that there is no danger. You have access to your neocortex and its connections to your emotional intelligence, relational skills, and emotional, social, and relational communication abilities. You have a sense of control.

. . . until you get triggered. In that moment the communication from your prefrontal cortex to your amygdala is interrupted. Dr. Daniel Siegel, a pioneer in the field of interpersonal neurobiology, calls it "flipping your lid."[2] Now the amygdala is in charge of what is happening. It signals danger and starts the activation of your brain and body into the fight, flight, or freeze response.

When you "flip your lid" you no longer have access to your emotional intelligence, your relational skills, your social understanding, or your communication skills. Your ability to make choices for good emotional interpersonal communication is gone. You are in a reactive state.

---

2 Dan Siegel, "'Flipping Your Lid': A Scientific Explanation," YouTube, February 28, 2012, https://www.youtube.com/watch?v=GoT_2NNoC68&t=66s

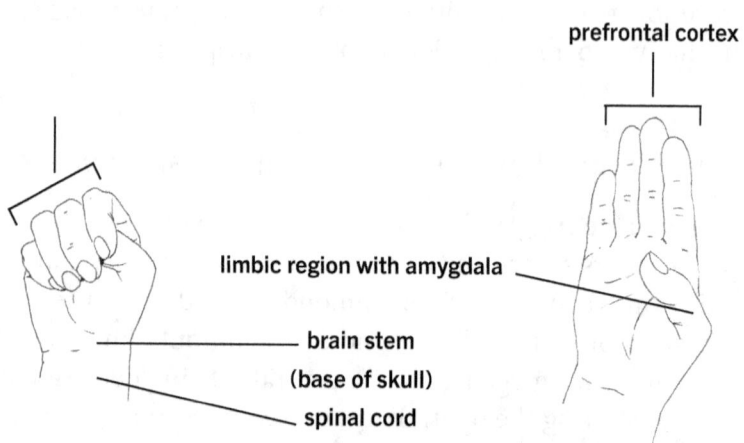

Flipping Your Lid

We are all very familiar with this state. You might have found yourself getting loud, swearing, saying mean things, maybe being aggressive, or just wanting to get away or disappear. You might have judged yourself afterward as being "bad," "wrong," or "unevolved" for the way you acted, behaved, or responded.

There was actually nothing wrong with you!

You just experienced the fight, flight, or freeze response being activated in your brain and body. This is a normal survival response—which most likely was not needed for your survival in that moment but was perceived as urgent and necessary by your brain!

Here in this chapter we talk about being triggered by perceived threats that are actually not dangerous.

When was the last time you were triggered? Did someone say something to you in a certain tone of voice or use a gesture that set you off? Did somebody ignore you? Or look at you in a certain way? Did you get angry and upset? Or maybe you got defensive and justified your position? Or did you pull away and get quiet? And your thoughts about the other person and maybe yourself and the situation, did they all become negative?

CHAPTER 9 | GETTING TRIGGERED

Most triggers happen through interactions with other people. When your brain perceives emotional danger, the other person is seen as the source of that danger and your brain turns them into the enemy! Most of the time, the other person means you no harm. Often they're already in a defensive and emotionally charged state themselves.

Evolutionarily, the fight, flight, or freeze response is an instinctual reaction to outer threats. When you get triggered by a *perceived* threat, you react from old feelings, thoughts, and **beliefs** you have about a situation from your past, a situation that was traumatic in some way. You *seem* to be reacting to an outer threat, but actually you are reacting to a limiting belief you learned through traumas in the past. **Your triggers are connected to your beliefs!**

The basic belief when getting triggered is: "I am not safe!" This can apply to not feeling safe physically, emotionally, sexually, energetically, or spiritually, depending on which memory of old experiences was awakened in you.

Let's look at how that plays out.

When you were growing up, you formed limiting beliefs through smaller of larger traumatic experiences in which your needs were not met. These limiting beliefs can turn into the source of your triggers.

Let's look at a few examples of how these limiting beliefs can get activated and trigger you:

- If someone tells you in a certain tone of voice what to do, a belief from when you were growing up that "I am not seen as capable" or "I am not good enough" might be activated.
- If somebody does not listen to you or interrupts you a lot when you share something, beliefs from when you were growing up such as "What I have to say does not matter,"

"My feelings and needs don't matter," or "I don't matter" might be activated.

- If you were physically or sexually abused when you were growing up, certain noises such as footsteps, a door slamming, or someone shouting can activate the belief "I am not safe."

> *It is your limiting beliefs that trigger you, not your old experiences! When you change the underlying meaning and beliefs of those experiences, you won't get triggered anymore! Even though the smaller and larger traumatic experiences of your past stay the same!*

When you are triggered, what's in the present is *reminding* you of something in the past. But actually, it's not the old experiences that you are reacting to but the *meaning you gave* those experiences. Being triggered really means you are reacting to your own limiting beliefs.

If you did not have limiting beliefs, you would not get triggered! Even if you had experiences in your childhood, when your needs to matter, to be seen, to be validated, to be supported, and to be safe were not met.

It is your limiting beliefs that trigger you, not your old experiences! When you change the underlying meaning and beliefs of those experiences, you won't get triggered anymore! Even though the smaller and larger traumatic experiences of your past stay the same!

When you are triggered, you feel hurt, upset, and afraid. You think you are being attacked and hurt by the other person. Your fight, flight, or freeze response makes you want to counter-attack, defend yourself, or run away and hide. But most of the time the other person does not actually mean to harm, hurt, or attack you. Why then do you feel so hurt, threatened, angry, and afraid? You feel that way because the old limiting belief that was activated *seemed to be confirmed* by the behaviour or words of the other person and you feel threatened *by that*. The other person's behaviour and words, or a situation, just activated those old limiting beliefs!

Being triggered feels very uncomfortable. You might feel small and powerless, afraid and threatened, hurt and unseen, or angry and enraged. Sometimes it can feel like the end of your world.

But even though being triggered feels so bad, there are gems to be found in these uncomfortable experiences. Being triggered offers a powerful opportunity to find and identify your limiting thoughts and beliefs. Without knowing these learned limiting beliefs you will end up re-experiencing the feelings, thoughts, and body sensations they create. You will get triggered and react over and over again in ways that don't feel good. When you know these limiting beliefs you can change them.

The ability to get to the gems of a trigger is a skill that needs to be learned and practised like any other skill. There is a Road Map for Navigating the Trigger Response and Getting to the Gems in Appendix 3. If you like, use that as a guideline when you are in a triggered state and need some support to shift out of it.

Here we are going through each step in detail.

How to navigate the trigger response and get to the gems

Become aware of your triggered state

Recognize, become aware that you are triggered

Know your trigger responses

- Notice your body symptoms
- Notice your feelings
- Notice your thoughts

When we are triggered, the amygdala sets into motion a fight, flight, or freeze response in our brain and body. Most of us go more readily to *one* of these three responses. When you know which one you have a tendency to go to, you have a better chance of noticing earlier on when you are triggered.

Each one has certain body symptoms, feelings, and thoughts that can become your signals.

Symptoms you might notice when you are in a **fight response**:

Body sensations

- Your heart is beating faster, stronger
- You're taking deep breaths
- Your vision is getting narrow and focused on the other person
- Your hands, face, or chest are getting sweaty
- You feel tense
- Your stomach feels like it's burning or in a knot
- Your face is tightening up
- Your hand is making a fist

- You feel like you want to punch, stomp, or kick

Feelings

- You feel scared
- You feel angry

Thoughts about the other person

- "You are so mean."
- "What an asshole."
- "You're so wrong."
- "I'll show you."
- "I hate you."

Symptoms you might notice when you are in a **flight response:**

Body sensations

- You feel tense
- You feel fidgety
- Your legs or feet are restless
- You look around a lot
- Your breathing is shallow

Feelings

- You are afraid
- You feel trapped

Thoughts about your situation

- "I am not safe."
- "I need to get out of here."

- "I need to get away."

... And when you are in a **freeze response:**

Body symptoms
- You're almost holding your breath
- Your heart is beating faster or slower
- You feel stiff or heavy
- You feel cold
- You feel numb
- Your body is contracting
- Your mind goes blank

Feelings
- You feel overwhelmed
- You can't quite make out your feelings
- Your feelings are numb or fuzzy
- You have a sense of dread
- You feel disconnected

Thoughts about your situation
- "I don't want to be seen."
- "This doesn't feel safe."
- "I don't want to be here."

One symptom that **all three responses** have in common is **the sense of urgency, the sense that you have to act right now!**

So, no matter which trigger response you experience, the sense of urgency is your clearest signal that you are triggered.

To find the trigger response you tend to go to, look at the symptoms in the lists above and see which ones are familiar to you. You can also take a moment and remember the last time you were triggered. What did you experience in:

- your body?
- your feelings?
- your thoughts?

You might notice that you also had body sensations, feelings, and thoughts that are not listed here.

In a real threatening situation and real danger, these responses can be lifesaving. With perceived threats, which we are talking about here, the trigger responses are not actually useful.

When you're experiencing the inner upset and emotional chaos of the fight, flight, or freeze response, when you are ready to yell, hit, run away, or disappear, it is not a good time to try to figure things out or communicate much with the person you were triggered by.

Why? Because you've "flipped your lid."

Your prefrontal cortex is no longer in charge. The connection between your prefrontal cortex and your amygdala has been interrupted. You don't have access to your neocortex functions anymore. With that you lose access to your emotional intelligence, your social understanding, and your communication skills.

> *The clearest signal that you are being triggered is your sense of urgency, the sense that you have to act right now.*

Let's explore the *sense of urgency,* the symptom all three trigger responses have in common, a bit more. If we look at it as an instinctual survival response, which the flight, flight, or freeze response is, urgency makes sense. This instinct makes you want to react, to run, to hide—immediately, *right now.* As an instinct it is meant to save your life, and that is why you experience a sense of urgency.

This urgency is hard to resist. When you are triggered it is really a challenge to not react. But no matter how strong your urge is to get loud or sharp; to defend, explain, or justify yourself; to run or hide, these reactions are rarely helping your communication. Remember, it is your amygdala talking in these moments, and your amygdala doesn't have any emotional intelligence or communication skills!

It is also very easy to get triggered when another person around you is triggered. You've probably experienced this. It is quite possible that mirror neurons are involved in creating this particular reaction. Mirror neurons exist in different parts of our brain. They let us mirror other people's behaviour and experience their feelings at the same time they experience them. So, if someone around you is in a triggered state, your mirror neurons could cause you to feel their feelings and mirror their behaviour. Even though you were calm a moment before, now you are in a triggered state as well.

Besides the possibility of your mirror neurons moving you suddenly into a trigger response in situations like that, you might also be reacting to your own past. For example, when someone around you is in a fight response and attacks and blames you, memories of being attacked, accused, or blamed might awaken in you. Or, if the triggered person goes into a flight or freeze response and "disappears" emotionally, it could bring up memories of feeling abandoned or of others being emotional unavailable to you when you needed them.

CHAPTER 9 | GETTING TRIGGERED

When two people are triggered at the same time, they could both be in a fight response. You are most likely familiar with that experience—when you and the other person end up going deeper and deeper into a fight, attacking, arguing, defending, and justifying. It's like two amygdalae are talking at each other!

Listening is not available to either of you. This makes so much sense when you see it as a survival instinct. Evolutionarily, imagine what would have happened if you had stopped to listen—you would have been eaten by that tiger!

You might also know how it feels when two people have different trigger responses. Let's say you are in a fight response and the other person is in a flight or freeze response. It feels like the other person just disappears, physically, emotionally, verbally, or energetically. You just can't reach them anymore. And you have a burning urge to argue and prove your point. You want to be heard so urgently, and the other person can't hear you! Remember how frustrating that feels?

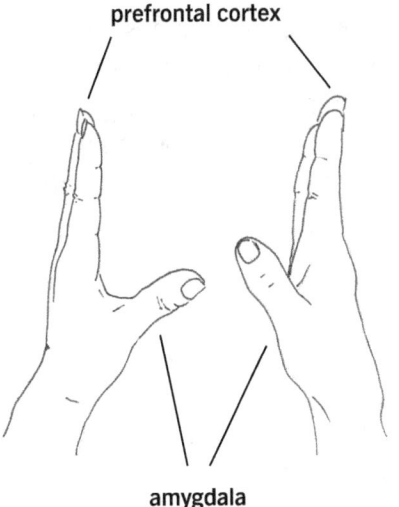

Two Amygdalae "Talking" to Each Other

Or you are the one who wants to disappear—physically, emotionally, verbally, or energetically—and the other person keeps "coming at you." You just want to feel safe, and the other person won't leave you alone. How frustrating that is!

To be able to consciously move out of your triggered state you first of all need to learn to recognize that you are triggered. Find a few body symptoms, feelings, and thoughts that are *your* particular trigger signals.

Your goal is to recognize when you are triggered. It takes practice. When you start out learning this, you might realize only afterward that you were triggered. As your awareness of being triggered grows, you might notice it more readily while you are in the middle of it. You watch your thoughts turn into mean words, you notice your impulse to walk out the door, or you become aware of your urge to explain and justify, and you realize, "I am triggered!" The more you practise noticing being triggered, the closer to the onset of the trigger you will recognize it.

Communicate that you are triggered, if appropriate

Before you take steps to calm your trigger response, decide if you need or want to communicate to the other person that you are triggered. If the trigger happened in your intimate relationship or with a close friend you are emotionally open with, it might be good to let the other person know that you are triggered and that you will take some time to get calm again.

You could say:

> "I got triggered and I need a bit of time to myself. Can we talk about this again this evening?"

> "I have so many emotions coming up right now. I need a bit of time to sort them out on my own. Let's check in with each other again in an hour."

> "I just need a bit of time and space for myself. I'm going for a walk. I'll be back in half an hour."

Basically, you let the other person know that you need space and time to yourself and that you'll be back.

You could bring up the issue of getting triggered with your partner or friend in a conversation when neither of you is reactive.

You can create some words, sentences, or signals that you agree to use when you are triggered. Since your emotional, social, and communicational intelligence is "out of order" when you are triggered, it can be helpful to have some prearranged communication in place for this situation.

If you are in a situation with people you are not that close to or emotionally open with, finding a way to leave the situation can be helpful. Excuse yourself for a moment, go to the washroom, or just move yourself out of the situation with no need for explanation.

Come to a calm state

Create time and space for yourself away from the triggering situation and person you got triggered by

When you recognize that you are triggered, create time and space for yourself away from the triggering situation, including the person you got triggered by. Find a way to leave the situation. Go to another room, go outside, take a bathroom break. When you get out of the triggering situation, your brain starts reading the situation as safe again. Your system starts to move toward calm because the perceived danger is gone.

Take the focus off the other person and bring it to yourself

This is hard to do. The trigger response causes you to see the other person as the enemy. It is easier to take the focus off the other person when you leave the situation. And even when you are physically away from the other person and situation, your brain still wants to think about it. It might try to explain and justify—it just can't let it go. What is fuelling these thoughts is actually not the other person or what just happened but your own limiting beliefs!

Come to calm when by yourself

Taking the following steps supports bringing the focus to yourself and will calm your system by balancing your brain again and relaxing your body.

- Feel your feet on the ground.

  Doing this moves you into body awareness. It slows down your brain waves and brings you into the present moment.

  You can follow this basic grounding practice: Bring your awareness to the soles of your feet. Feel them touching the inside of your shoes and the floor. Sense and imagine the floor being connected to the Earth. Through that, sense your feet being connected to the Earth. Let your breath be slow and gentle while you do this.

- Take deep breaths into your belly.

  It can be helpful to put your hands on your belly and breathe into the space underneath your hands. Feel or see your hands move up and down with your breath. After you take a deep breath into your belly, you can hold it there for a moment and then have a long, slow breath out. Breathing into your belly activates the parasympathetic part of your autonomous nervous system. This helps you slow down and bring the body to calm. The parasympathetic autonomous nervous system is active when you sleep, relax, and digest, and is necessary for healing.

  Conversely, breathing into your upper body activates the sympathetic part of your autonomic nervous system, which is already highly activated when you are triggered. It is that part that gets you ready for action.

- Hold yourself in compassion and give yourself empathy
  - Verbal self-compassion and self-empathy.

Here are sentences you could say to yourself:

"This was really hard."
"I am really upset/sad/angry/frustrated . . ."

Offer yourself comforting thoughts, such as:
"Things will be okay."
"Even though I am really upset right now, I will be okay."

Dan Siegel created the phrase "name it to tame it."[3] Naming and acknowledging your feelings without judging yourself for them calms the hyperactivity of the right side of your brain. It helps to create more balance between the right and left hemispheres of the brain. It calms the amygdala. It helps to get the prefrontal cortex back in charge.

- Nonverbal self-compassion and self-empathy.

Here are things you can do:

Stroke your chest, arms, belly, and face. Make cooing sounds, just as you would with a young child.

Doing an extended grounding exercise is really helpful, particularly after you have calmed down a bit already—in other words, after you have given yourself some verbal self-empathy: Feel your feet connected to the Earth as in the previous grounding exercise. Then imagine growing energetic roots from your feet down into the soil of the Earth, just like tree roots. Allow the Earth to bring the nurturing, supportive, caring, and loving energies she has for you and your body into these roots. Let these energies move to all the places in your body that need to be calmed right now. Let the nurturing, support, care, and love touch and fill these places. When you feel it's enough, bring your focus to your

---

3   Dan Siegel, "Name It to Tame It," YouTube, December 8, 2014, https://www.youtube.com/watch?v=ZcDLzppD4Jc

heart and thank the Earth for her nurturing, support, care, and love for you and your body.

- Do some physical exercise.

  Walk, run, work in your garden, stack or chop firewood. Physical exercise uses up the adrenaline that is rushing through your body—the adrenaline that was getting your body ready to fight or flee.

- Use EFT (Emotional Freedom Technique) to calm your emotions.

  Tap on the tapping points while saying out loud statements about your feelings, body sensations, thoughts, and the situation you were in. This will help your body come back to calm. (See chapter 11, The Basics of Tapping.)

- Engage in activities that are caring for yourself and your surroundings.

  Listen to music. Do the extended version of grounding your body. Weed your garden. Clean your house. Wash your car.

Again, activity will give your brain the signal that the situation is safe now and your body can move into calm.

Find the gems

Identify the needs that were not met for you in the triggering situation

When you feel calm again in your body and in your emotions, the other person will seem less of a threat to you. Your calmness allows for the possibility of realizing that they might actually not be your enemy. When you notice this, take your focus off the other person even more and become curious about your needs that have not been met.

When you get triggered, there are always needs that are not being met—or *it seems to you* they are not being met.

Let's look at this in a few examples.

You share something honestly in a meeting and then someone looks at you in a certain way and you get triggered.

- Your need to feel emotionally safe when you express yourself was not being met.

Someone makes a suggestion about how to improve a situation you are in and you feel criticized and get triggered.

- Your need to feel capable and good enough was not being met.
- Your need to feel valued for who you are was not being met.

You get interrupted by someone a few times in a row and you get triggered.

- Your need for respect was not being met.
- Your need to matter was not being met.

A war veteran hears a door slamming. His memory associates the bang of the door with the sound of a gunshot and he gets triggered.

- His need for safety was not met.

You share something in a group of friends and one of them says, "No, no, it's not like that," and you get triggered.

- Your needs to be understood, to be validated, to matter, and to be seen are not met.

Sometimes the fight, flight, or freeze response is not sudden but can be built up by the story we tell ourselves about an experience or situation. This is fuelled by the needs that are not being met and by the beliefs we have.

Let's look at this in a few examples again.

Your partner said she will be home at a certain time. She doesn't show up when she said she would and doesn't let you know that she'll be late. You run all sorts of scenarios in your head, trying to explain why she is not home yet . . . and then she turns up looking cheerful, sharing that she had run into a friend and they started talking. You get triggered.

- Your needs for consideration, for acknowledgement, to matter, and to be seen were not met.

You wrote an email or text to a friend. You asked if he could help you with something. Then you don't hear from your friend for days. You are starting to get triggered. In this kind of trigger, you don't experience a complete "flipping your lid," but more a "fluttering of your lid."

- You are starting to think and feel that your need for support, communication, and connection is not being not met.

You might wonder, "Why do I get triggered only in certain situations? Sometimes, even though my needs aren't met, I *don't* get triggered at all. Why is that?"

You only get triggered when you have a limiting belief about a need! When a need is not met but you don't have a limiting belief connected to it, you don't get triggered.

Find and identify your thoughts and beliefs about the unmet needs

You get triggered because the unmet needs of the triggering situation are linked to a limiting belief. That limiting belief basically tells you, "You can't have that need fulfilled."

Let's go through the examples of those unmet needs again and see what limiting beliefs might be underlying them.

You share something honestly in a meeting and someone looks at you a certain way.

- Looking through the perspective of a limiting belief, you interpret the look as criticism, rejection, or disapproval. While actually the other person might have made a certain face as they were trying to understand what you are saying. When you were growing up, you were often criticized and disapproved of when you shared your true feelings and thoughts. You formed the belief "I am not safe to express who I really am." This old belief was activated and triggered you.

Someone makes a suggestion to you about how to improve a situation you are in.

- You feel criticized because you perceive it through a belief like "I am not capable," "I am not good enough," "Others criticize me," or "I am not valued for what I do."

You get interrupted a few times in a row when you are trying to explain something.

- You experience it through beliefs like "Nobody respects me," "I am not worthy to be respected," "What I have to say does not matter," or "I don't matter."

A war veteran gets triggered by a loud door bang. A fear of getting shot gets activated.

- It is connected to the belief "I am not safe."

You share something in a group of friends, and one of them says, "No, no, it's not like that." And you get triggered.

- You experience the situation through the beliefs "My reality does not matter," "Others dismiss me," and "I don't matter."

Your partner comes home later than she said she would. When she finally arrives home looking cheerful, you end up being triggered.

- Beliefs that were activated and triggered you might sound like "Others don't consider me," "What I feel and need does not matter," "I am not important to others," "I am not cared about," or "I can't trust others."

You wrote an email or text to a friend. You asked if he could help you with something. You don't hear from your friend for days and are starting to feel a bit triggered. You experience a "fluttering of your lid."

- You are wondering why your friend has not responded and you might have thoughts like, "Maybe I am asking for too much," or "Maybe my friend does not like me anymore, because I asked for too much." The more you listen to these thoughts, the more you activate your limiting beliefs. Beliefs like, "When I ask for what I want, I am too much—I am being a burden," "When I ask for what I want, others don't want to be with me and I get abandoned," or "No one is there for me." Through these interpretations of the missing response from your friend you activated your limiting beliefs. Now you "flipped your lid" and are in a triggered reaction.

As uncomfortable and challenging as getting triggered is, it can be the super-highway to find and identify your limiting beliefs. The hard part in the beginning is to let go of blaming the other person for how you feel. It is really important to shift into being curious about your needs and your beliefs about them.

Gently ask yourself, "Which of my need(s) were not met?" Was it your need for safety, to matter, to be seen, to be loved, to be supported, to be cared for, to be respected? Use the list of needs to help you identify your unmet needs.

And when you find these needs, ask yourself what you believe about these needs. "What do I believe that I feel so hurt?" "What do I believe about these needs that were not met?" These questions, when asked with gentleness and compassion for yourself, will help you find those limiting beliefs that were activated and triggered you.

Shift the limiting beliefs

State your limiting beliefs

You might find limiting beliefs like these:

"I don't matter."

"My feelings and needs don't matter."

"No one cares about me."

"I am not safe."

"I am not worthy to be loved/to be supported/to be respected."

"I am not good enough" (or a variation of this).

Find a sentence for your belief that really resonates with you. You might need to change a word here and there. You will feel an inner "Yes, that's it!" when the words of your belief statement are just right for you.

Dissolve the limiting beliefs

Give yourself understanding, compassion, and empathy for the smaller and larger traumatic experiences that caused the limiting belief.

Here are tools you can use to dissolve the limiting belief(s) that triggered you:

- EFT

  Tapping is a powerful tool to dissolve your limiting belief. It's described in detail in Part II.

- The "What-If process"

  You can also use the "What-if process" to weaken the power of the limiting belief you found. (See chapter 18, The Power of "What If . . . " and How to Ask Questions That Move You Forward, for more on this.)

Note: This process of navigating your trigger response and finding the gems is only for *perceived* danger. This process does NOT apply when you are in real danger and your fight, flight, or freeze response is activated. In real danger your fight, flight, or freeze response is there to protect you, to keep you safe, and to ensure your survival!

Results of using the steps of navigating the trigger response and getting to the gems

The moment you dissolve your limiting belief in your subconscious programming, the very same situation, behaviour, or words of the other person will *not* trigger you anymore.

However, a *similar* situation could still trigger you. In that case, another limiting belief got activated. It could also be a variation of the belief you cleared. If that happens, go through the same

CHAPTER 9 | GETTING TRIGGERED

process of finding the need, finding the limiting belief, and clearing the belief.

The more often you experience that you *can* find and clear your limiting belief when you get triggered, the more you will feel okay about getting triggered. And when you learn these skills and experience your ability to change your beliefs, the more you might welcome getting triggered as an opportunity to clear untrue beliefs about yourself.

You will notice that over time, the more limiting beliefs you clear, the less you get triggered.

You are on the road to emotional freedom. On the road back to your wholeness. You are coming back to living more from your innate sacredness and who you really are.

PART II

Dissolving Your Limiting Beliefs

Limiting beliefs
—like all beliefs—
are learned.

What has been learned can be unlearned.

Maybe you have already tried many times to let go of a limiting belief. You might have thought or said out loud what you'd like to believe instead. And you might have felt quite excited about it at first.

And then, after a while, you noticed that you have the same old thoughts, feelings, body sensations, behaviours, and experiences again, driven by the old limiting belief you intended to change—and you might have felt frustrated, upset, and defeated.

Why couldn't you change that belief?

Limiting beliefs from all the different sources we've discussed got programmed into your subconscious while you were in alpha or theta brainwave states as a child.

When you are in a rational and linear thinking state, your brain functions in beta frequencies. When you decide to change your limiting belief, and you think and say a new, different belief with your logical, linear mind alone, your brain is still in beta.

A rational thought and decision in a beta brainwave state cannot reprogram a limiting belief by itself. . . . For the actual reprogramming of your belief you need to communicate in the language of your subconscious.

In order to change a program, you need to use the right programming language. You cannot change the alpha or theta brainwave state programs of your subconscious by using the language of your beta brainwave states. If you could change your beliefs about your worthiness, your good-enoughness, or your lovability intellectually, you would have done so already.

It is similar to working on the computer—you need to use the appropriate programming language to change the program.

When I was less technically literate with word processing than I am now, I found myself trying to change my text from bullet points back to regular text. I would try to start the line at the left-hand margin only to get frustrated when it jumped back to being a bullet point. I would go down a few lines and try there, but again the text would jump back to the old layout. It wasn't that I was bad at typing—I just didn't know how to use the word processor properly to make the changes I wanted to make. I wasn't speaking the language of its program.

The same is true for changing limiting beliefs. There is nothing wrong with you if you haven't been able to change your limiting beliefs. You are not bad, wrong, or lacking in willpower. You just haven't been using the right programming language yet.

Your limiting beliefs were programmed into your subconscious while you were in an alpha or theta brainwave state.

A rational thought and decision in a beta brainwave state cannot reprogram a limiting belief by itself. A rational thought and decision can motivate you to take action to change your belief.

For the actual reprogramming of your belief you need to communicate in the language of your subconscious.

Methods that use the language of the subconscious and connect to the alpha and theta brainwave states are becoming more mainstream. They include:

- Emotional Freedom Technique (EFT)
- Eye Movement Desensitization and Reprocessing (EMDR)
- Hypnosis
- Psych-K
- Subliminal Messaging
- Theta Healing

These are all useful methods for dissolving limiting beliefs and updating your conditioned programs.

In this book I focus on the process of dissolving limiting beliefs by using the Emotional Freedom Technique.

We update our computers, tablets, and cell phones frequently. And yet most of us run our lives on outdated belief programs that are twenty, thirty, forty, fifty, or sixty years old and were created by our 3-, 4-, 5-, 6-, or 7-year-old selves!

The next chapters give you detailed information on updating old limiting belief programs and guide you how to do it. If you would like to be supported by a practitioner in this process, look for someone who uses subconscious reprogramming methods and whose personal energy, language, and style resonate with you!

Chapter 10

An Introduction to the Emotional Freedom Technique

Emotional Freedom Technique (EFT), also known as tapping, is a therapy method from the field of energy psychology. The use of this powerful and effective tool of choice in counselling and therapy sessions is expanding into schools, hospitals, and homes.

In EFT, you tap with one or more fingers on meridian (acupuncture) points on your hands, face, and upper body while saying statements relating to your physical, emotional, and mental experiences.

Over decades the method developed into its current form through the work of practitioner pioneers including Dr. George Goodheart (US chiropractor), Dr. John Diamond, MD (Australian psychiatrist), Dr. Roger Callahan (US psychologist), Gary Craig (US NLP and EFT practitioner), Dr. Patricia Carrington (US psychologist), and Dawson Church, PhD, among others. Nick Ortner and Jessica Ortner have contributed greatly to tapping becoming more mainstream.

In 2013 I came across EFT through the online Tapping World Summit, produced by Nick and Jessica Ortner. I listened to every single tapping session during those ten days and wrote down every word of all the sessions verbatim. I tried it out for myself for months after. I learned how it feels inside, what makes it work, and what doesn't.

One day, I was tapping on a severe past-life trauma I had tried to heal for some time. So far nothing had worked. But in that tapping sequence something shifted and a significant aspect of that past-life trauma healed. Now I was convinced. I started to use EFT in sessions with my clients. Today it is one of my most important tools. I also teach it to my clients so they can learn to use it on their own. It is one of the most effective and powerful tools that I know for healing trauma and dissolving limiting beliefs.

Much of what I share with you about tapping in the following chapters comes from my personal experiences and my experiences as a counsellor in guiding others through the tapping process.

You might have experienced many times how hard it is to shift emotional states, memories, body sensations, behavioural patterns, and beliefs through rational thoughts alone.

> *One of the first effects of tapping is a reduction of the stress response. It signals safety to the nervous system.*

When using EFT, you communicate with the subconscious programming in you that creates and influences your emotional states, memories, body sensations, behavioural patterns, and beliefs. Using EFT, you communicate with the alpha/theta program within you.

While you tap with your fingers on the acupuncture points, you say statements about your:

- feelings,
- body sensations,
- memories,
- thoughts,
- energies, and
- beliefs.

Often, the reason you find specific experiences challenging is that the limbic system of your brain has categorized and labelled those experiences as threatening and unwanted. If an experience in the present resembles something in the past that has been labelled "threatening," "dangerous," or "not safe," that part of your brain gets activated and your emotions and your body go into a stress response. One of the first effects of tapping is a reduction of this stress response. It signals safety to the nervous system. The limbic system moves out of danger mode. Your emotions and body calm down. Often people notice and say after a few rounds of tapping, "I feel calmer." Studies have shown that cortisol levels drop after tapping.[4]

The moment the stress response is reduced, your emotions, your body reactions, your thoughts, your energies, and your beliefs can reorganize themselves. Using EFT is a powerful way to support this reorganization by communicating with the subconscious.

---

4   Donna Bach et al., "Clinical EFT (Emotional Freedom Techniques) Improves Multiple Physiological Markers of Health," *Journal of Evidence-Based Medical Integration*, 24 (2019), https://www.ncbi.nlm.nih.gov/pmc/articles/PMC6381429

The moment the stress response is reduced, your emotions, your body reactions, your thoughts, your energies, and your beliefs can reorganize themselves. Using EFT is a powerful way to support this reorganization by communicating with the subconscious.

Chapter 11

The Basics of Tapping

If you are fairly new to tapping, here is a short introduction to general tapping steps.

Use the EFT Tapping Point Chart at the end of this chapter for the tapping points.

Tapping steps

Decide what you want to tap on.

You can tap on a feeling, a body sensation or body pain, a situation, repeating thoughts you have, or a belief—most likely all these are connected to old traumas. Create a statement about it. For example:

"I feel so anxious" (feeling).

"I feel tension and pain in my shoulder" (body sensation/pain).

"When my sister ignored me, I felt so upset and angry" (situation and feelings).

"I often think that I don't know how to do things" (repeating thoughts).

"I am not good enough" (belief).

Rate the intensity of your statement.

Give your statement a rating number of 0 to 10. A rating of 0 means the statement is not true for you. A rating of 10 means it is very true for you. Go with your gut feeling. Use the first rating that comes to mind.

Tap the set-up statement on the karate chop point.

Your set-up statement is your statement of the feeling, body sensation, situation, thought, or belief you chose, combined with a statement of acceptance, kindness, or gentleness toward yourself.

For example, "Even though . . . (I feel so anxious/I feel this pain in my shoulder), I choose to love and accept myself/I can be kind to myself/I choose to be gentle with myself." (See chapter 12, How to Tap to Dissolve Limiting Beliefs, for more information on the set-up statement.)

When you have created your set-up statement, tap it three times on the karate chop point.

Tap your chosen statement on points 2–9.

Say your chosen statement at each point, moving from point 2 to point 9. We call this tapping a round.

At the end of the round, check in with yourself.

Take a deep breath into your belly and breathe out slowly. Then check in with yourself: "How am I feeling? What body sensations am I noticing? What thoughts am I aware of? Is a memory coming up? Do I notice an image? What do I notice energetically?"

The responses you get in your check-in are the answers from your subconscious to your tapping.

Continue by tapping another round on points 2–9.

For your next round of tapping you can use a statement that holds information from your check-in, or you can use your original statement from the beginning again. Choose whatever resonates most with you.

Continue with tapping rounds.
Do check-ins after your rounds.

When you tap a sequence of statements, you might feel ready to stop and do a check-in after one round. It can also take two or three rounds, occasionally more, for you to feel "now is the time to stop and do a check-in." Go with your feeling sense about it.

After a few rounds, do another rating of your original statement.

If your rating is above 5, continue tapping on what you are feeling, remembering and thinking, or sensing in your body, or on your beliefs. If your rating has dropped to 5 or lower, you can shift to tapping on new choices of feelings, body sensations, pain, thoughts, and beliefs.

Tapping a new choice.

You can tap, for example, "I feel less anxious and more relaxed," "I can choose to let go of this pain," "When I think of the old situation, I feel more confident," "I can allow myself more and more to trust that I am good enough."

Test this new choice.

Think of what usually brings up those old feeling, body sensations, pain, thoughts, or belief—the messages of your inner experiences of past trauma.

- If the intensity of your old inner experience does *not* go up, hurray! You are ready to move into living your new choice that you tapped.
- If the intensity of your feeling, body sensation, pain, thoughts, or belief goes up again, there is more to tap on.

Tap on statements that hold information that came up when you tested your new choice.

- If the rating stays above 5, listen very closely to the feedback from your subconscious through your check-ins.

Some aspects of your experience might still want to be addressed. (For more on this, see the next chapter.)

When to stop the tapping process, even if it is not "done."

- You are getting too tired.
- You are running out of time.
- You have no private space anymore.
- You feel overwhelmed or uncomfortable with what comes up emotionally.

If you find yourself in any of these situations, you can choose to end your tapping process anytime. You can do that by tapping statements like:

"I am getting too tired."

"I am running out of time."

"I choose to stop here."

"I allow myself to gently put it aside for now."

"I hold myself in acceptance, gentleness, and kindness."

"I am closing this for now and will come back to it another time."

"I feel overwhelmed by what is coming up. These are big emotions to experience on my own. I don't know how to tap on this on my own. I choose to stop here, and I hold myself in acceptance, gentleness, and kindness. I will look for someone who is experienced with tapping, who can be with me, guide me, and support me in tapping through this. I will continue the process with their support."

After you have tapped statements like these, stop tapping and take a few deep belly breaths and long, slow breaths out. Feel your feet on the ground.

If you have not experienced tapping before and you would like more support when you try it, you can use introductory online tapping videos. Books on tapping are a great source of information. You might also consider some sessions with a tapping practitioner to get familiar and comfortable with the process.

EFT Tapping Points Chart

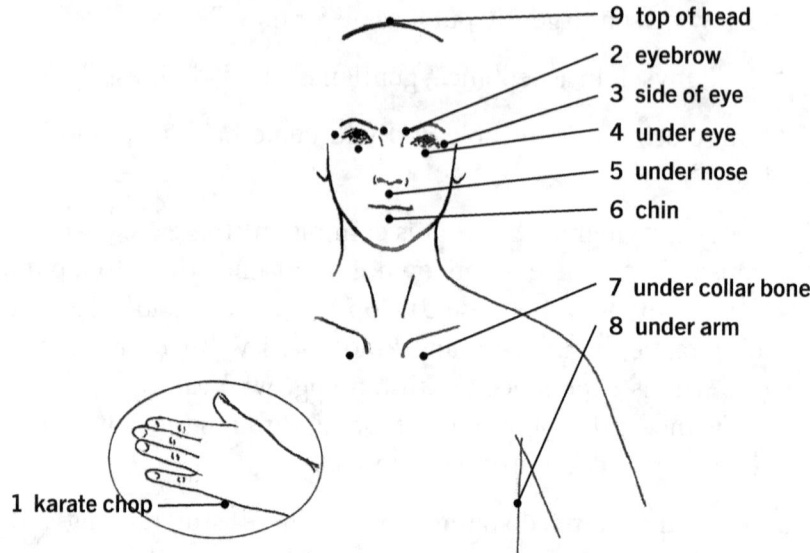

Chapter 12

How to Tap to Dissolve Limiting Beliefs

"How do I find the right sentence to start my tapping with?" you might wonder.

In the process of forming a limiting belief, you experienced certain body sensations, feelings, and thoughts in response to the smaller or larger traumatic experiences in family, school, social, and institutional situations you were in. Any of those body sensations, feelings, or thoughts you remember or re-experience can become the first sentence you use in your tapping sequence. You can also start by tapping on an unfulfilled need, dream, or goal you have been struggling with. You can use a trigger you experienced for your first tapping sentences as well. All of these connect you to your limiting beliefs.

Tapping is not a linear process where you go logically and directly from point A to point B. In your tapping process you want to hold a gentle curiosity about your belief and an openness to the possibility of it changing without you having a linear path in mind of how to get there. You want to allow the inner wisdom of your being, the part of you that knows the truth about you, to take the lead.

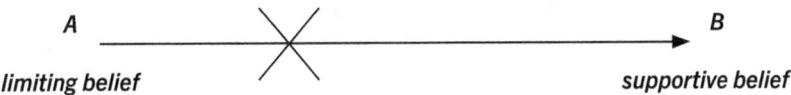

A
limiting belief

B
supportive belief

Even though the linear path looks like the shorter path, you might end up pushing, exerting effort, and struggling. When you push for a fast, direct end result, all the subconscious information connected to that limiting belief—the old situations, feelings, body sensations, thoughts, and the larger context of that limiting belief—is not addressed. The subconscious information will pull you back to your limiting belief when you push for a fast result. This push and pull creates struggle and exertion. And it just doesn't work.

Your subconscious wisdom will most likely take you on a winding path.

A
limiting belief

B
supportive belief

Your subconscious wisdom knows the feelings, body sensations, thoughts, memories, and energies that are connected to your limiting beliefs. It knows what sequence to follow to address them. What you notice during your check-in gives you the information from your subconscious for your next round of tapping. Even though following the lead of your subconscious wisdom appears to take longer, in the long run it will take less effort and less time to dissolve your limiting beliefs.

With that in mind, you are ready to start your tapping journey!

You'll find a summary of the tapping steps in Appendix 4.

Tapping steps

Set-up statement
You want to start your tapping sequence by tapping on what is present in the moment without pushing for change. This is expressed in the set-up statement. Here you combine what is

challenging for you with a statement of acceptance and kindness. When you tap on a challenging experience *and* move into kindness, nonjudgment, acceptance, and love for yourself, the limbic system in your brain registers more safety and calms down. It registers that there is nothing that urgently needs to change in order for you to be safe because you are already accepted, loved, and held in kindness.

You can start with either:

1. a statement of a feeling, body sensation, situation, thought, or an unfulfilled need, dream, or goal, or

2. a statement of a limiting belief you are aware of.

Use whichever one you choose for the set-up statement and add a statement of acceptance and kindness. Tap it on the karate chop point. For example:

1. "Even though I often feel anxious when I am in a group of people, I choose/can choose/can learn to be gentle and kind to myself."

"Even though I feel less than others, I choose to be/I am gentle and loving with myself."

"Even though I am scared to speak up with my friend, I choose/can choose/can learn to love and accept myself."

Or:

2. "Even though I believe what I have to say does not count, I choose/can choose/can learn to be gentle and kind to myself."

"Even though I believe that I am less than others, I choose to be/I am gentle and loving with myself."

"Even though I believe that if I speak up with my friend, I will be rejected, I choose/can choose/can learn to love and accept myself."

It might be tempting to say, "Even though I am scared to speak up with my friend, I choose to be confident to do so." This is actually not a statement of acceptance. It is already a possible outcome that the tapping process might lead you to later on.

When you create your set-up statements, let go of looking for solutions to what you are struggling with. Right now, it is about acceptance of the situation. Acceptance of what you feel and experience. Acceptance of and kindness for yourself.

Let's look at why this is so important.

You might have experienced that when you push against something in your life, you actually create a closer relationship with it.

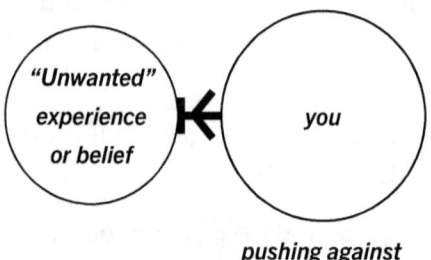

pushing against

Or maybe you are very focused on wanting to figure out an emotional challenge. Figuring out what needs to be understood and what needs to change has its place. But when your figuring-out comes from resisting what is, from wanting so badly to feel different, or from just being impatient, you end up adding energy to the unwanted experience and circumstances. You get into a closer relationship with what you are trying to figure out and get stuck in it.

CHAPTER 12 | HOW TO TAP TO DISSOLVE LIMITING BELIEFS

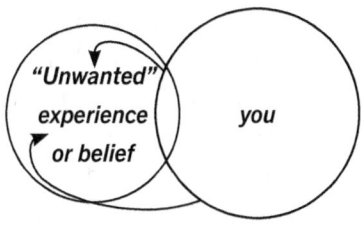

trying to figure out

But when your figuring-out comes from open curiosity, acceptance of what is, acceptance of yourself in this moment, then you create more space between what you want to change and yourself.

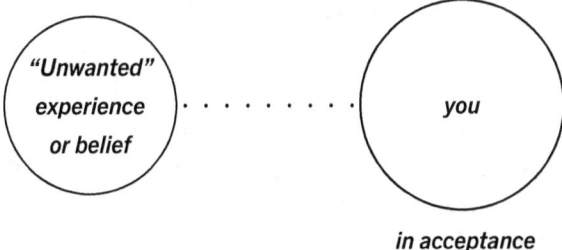

in acceptance

This is what happens when you say your set-up statement.

You create what in Buddhism is called *detachment.* When you create space between you and the challenging experience or limiting belief, there is room for change. Allow yourself to trust that whatever is challenging will change in this process and come to a place that feels better.

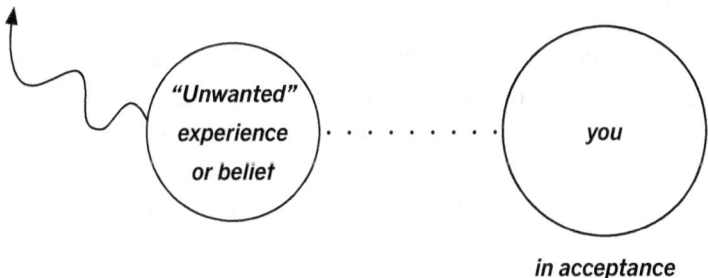

in acceptance

The figuring-out of the elements and complexity of what you are tapping on will happen naturally as you listen to your check-ins. Your subconscious will do the figuring-out for you. Your job is to listen to its messages, which show up as feelings, body sensations, energies, memories, images, and thoughts. Your job is to listen to these messages with openness, curiosity, and acceptance and then use them for your tapping sentences.

For example, by tapping on the set-up statement "Even though I am scared to speak up with my friend, I choose to be gentle and kind with myself," you create space between what is challenging to you and yourself.

It is important that while you are saying it, you *feel* what your words are expressing. In order to be able to feel your statement of acceptance, you need to choose exactly the the right words for you. You can adapt these statements of acceptance—"I accept and love myself," "I am gentle and kind with myself," "I am kind with myself," "I am gentle and loving with myself"— by adding these little words: "I can . . . ," "I could . . . ," "I can choose to . . . ," "I can learn to . . . " For example, "I *can learn* to accept and love myself."

After you have tapped your set-up statement three times at the karate chop point, continue with tapping rounds. But now you use only the first part of your set-up statement and leave out the statement of acceptance while you tap on points 2-9.

Tapping until you find your limiting belief

If you start with a statement of your feelings, body sensations, thoughts, an unfulfilled need, dream, or goal, keep in mind that you want to get to the cause, the source of your experience—in other words, your limiting beliefs. Go with what feels emotionally important or charged, but not so charged that you feel overwhelmed.

Stay curious about the underlying beliefs. Ask yourself, "What must I believe that . . . "

"I feel this?"

"I think this?"

"I sense this?"

"I experience this?"

See also the questions in chapter 6, How Do You Find Your Beliefs?

It could be that you have an idea of what your belief is, but when you say it out loud it doesn't sound quite right yet. Keep tapping on your belief statement as it is right now and change the wording of it as you go through the tapping points. Change the belief statement bit by bit. At some point it will "click." You will feel an emotional connection to your belief statement when you find exactly the right wording.

Rate your belief

When you find your belief, give it a feeling rating on a scale of 0 to 10, where 0 = feels not true, and 10 = feels fully true. Remember, you might not believe this belief intellectually, but in your subconscious programming it is true. Rate your belief from your felt sense.

The rating is there to guide you in your tapping process. Go with the rating number that comes up first without judging it. There is no right or wrong number for your rating. What is important is that it comes from your feeling sense and *not your thinking*.

Your rating numbers help you decide when to move on to the next tapping step. Here is how they guide you in your tapping process:

- If the intensity of your rating number drops, it shows you that you are on the right track with your tapping statements.

- If it does not drop for several tapping rounds, it shows that you might be circling, that there is another issue connected to what you are tapping on that still needs to be addressed.

- If it goes up, it shows you that you opened another charged issue that is related to the limiting belief you are tapping on.

It is not crucial to rate your belief in order to dissolve your limiting belief. The more experienced you are in tapping and the more you trust your own feeling sense, the less often you actually need to rate your belief. Then you are able to let the felt intensity or ease of feelings guide you without giving it a rating number.

Tapping on the statement of the belief

Say the belief while you tap on the tapping points 2–9. Here are some possible statements you could say:

"I have the belief that I am not good enough."

"I believe that I am not good enough."

"I learned to believe that I am not good enough."

"I have this old belief that I am not good enough."

Tapping on inner experiences that come up for you around this belief

Tap on feelings, body sensations, memories, thoughts, energies, images—any context that comes up around this belief. Go through the tapping points while saying out loud statements about the feelings, body sensations, and thoughts you have, energies you sense, images you see, memories that come up that are related to this belief.

While you tap, have part of you hold yourself, your experience, and your feelings in acceptance, empathy, and kindness—while another part of you can be sad, mad, resistant, frustrated, hopeless, furious, confused . . . feeling all the different feelings you might be experiencing.

Tapping on how this belief came into your life

- You made meaning of your traumatic experiences as a child.
- You "absorbed" it from the people around you or "inherited" it from the people before you.

Here is a formula you can use to tap on how you made meaning of your traumatic childhood experiences.

The situation

"When my mom . . . (didn't protect me)."

"When my dad . . . (put me down)."

"When my brother, sister . . . (didn't include me)."

"When the teacher . . . (called me stupid)."

"When the kids at school . . . (laughed at me)."

Your feelings

"I felt sad, upset, afraid, scared, terrified, lonely, lost, mad, angry, confused . . ."

Your needs

"I needed to be heard, to be protected, to be held, to be supported, to be included, to be seen and understood . . . and there was no one there for me."

> "There was my grandma/neighbour/aunt/uncle/teacher who was there for me . . . and I felt safe/comforted/acknowledged/heard/supported, but I did not feel this with my parents/with my siblings/in school."

Forming the limiting belief

> "And so, I made meaning out of this. I gave it the meaning that I am not wanted/ I am not lovable/I don't deserve what I want/I am less than others/I am not good enough/ I am not worthy/I don't matter."

Give empathy, understanding, and acknowledgement to yourself for forming your belief

> "And this belief was true when I grew up. It makes so much sense that I would have thought this. There was no one there who told me the truth about what was going on. There was no one there to tell me that how my parents/my siblings/my teachers/other kids behaved was not about me. No one told me that my parents/my siblings/my teacher/other kids behaved that way because of what was going on for them."

For example, maybe there was no one who told you that your mother being depressed had nothing to do with you. It makes sense that, as a child, you would have thought that your feelings and needs didn't matter because she didn't pay attention to you. It makes sense that you would have formed the belief "My feelings and needs don't matter."

Or, when your sister was born, your mom paid so much attention to the new little baby. Everyone who came for a visit wanted to see the baby and said how beautiful she was. No one said how beautiful or amazing you were. You were praised for now being a proud older brother or sister, but you didn't really feel proud. You started to think you were not important anymore. You formed beliefs of unworthiness and not being loved.

So, tap, giving empathy to yourself for having experienced that.

Tap on empathy statements about what was missing for you (your unmet needs).

Tap, giving yourself empathy for having created that meaning.

Tap, giving yourself empathy for the fact that there was no one there who explained the situation, and so you gave meaning to it from the understanding you had as a 3-, 4-, 5-, 6-, or 7-year-old.

Here is what to focus on when you tap on how you "absorbed" the limiting belief from the people around you or "inherited" it from the people before you.

Tap on the larger context of the absorbed or inherited limiting belief.

- Your mother or father had the same belief.
- The belief came from your ancestral lineage, from the trauma of someone in previous generations.
- It was a collective belief of society and culture at the time of your upbringing.
- It was a religious belief of the church or religious group you were influenced by when you were growing up.

Become more and more aware of this larger context of your belief. Formulate sentences about it. Tap those sentences on the tapping points.

Make sure part of you comes from empathy, understanding, caring, and unconditional love for yourself and humanity, while another part of you can be sad, angry, frustrated, or upset—feeling all the feelings that come up for you.

It might sound like some of these statements:

"No wonder I have this belief. My mother has the same belief. And actually, my grandmother and great-grandmother had the same belief, and when I think about it, most likely generations of women before them had the same belief as well. It makes so much sense that I inherited this limiting belief."

"No wonder I have this belief. My father has the same belief. And when I think about it, my grandfather and great-grandfather had the same belief. And it is most likely that generations of men before them had the same belief as well. It makes so much sense that I inherited this limiting belief."

"I was a little kid, and of course I absorbed what was around me. I was the 'little sponge' that we are as children."

"This belief is so old. It was created generations ago. Maybe it served a good purpose when it was created. Maybe it was an interpretation of experiences by some little children back then. Maybe someone back then experienced a trauma. And out of that trauma this belief was formed."

"And this belief was passed on from generation to generation. And now I too have this belief. The lives of so many women/men were influenced and limited by this belief. I am sad, upset, angry, and frustrated about it."

Make sure you tap on the feelings you have about how this belief has affected so many people.

When the emotional charge of that has lessened, continue with statements like these:

"Maybe this belief is not needed anymore. It is possible that it's not needed anymore."

"(Maybe) I can be the person who is able to change this belief. The women/men of the generations before me didn't have the tools I have today. What if I choose to be the one changing this belief for all the women/men in my lineage? What if changing this belief could be my contribution to my well-being and the well-being of the people coming after me? Maybe it will also contribute to the well-being/healing of the people before me."

You might notice that when you tap on statements like these, you feel or sense a connection to the generations before you. You might sense that even though you experience this belief as something personal, it is also a belief and experience that is way bigger and older than you.

Allow yourself to sense what your ancestors would say about you changing this inherited belief. You could ask them directly in your mind and heart. Most often, when people do this, they say, "I sense that my ancestors would like me to be happy. I sense that they agree to me letting go of this limiting belief. They would like that."

When you are done tapping on the statements relating to the absorbing/inheriting of the limiting belief, and when you are done tapping on the understanding of the larger context, you might feel an inner settledness and sense of peace.

Tapping on regret and grief relating to the limiting belief

Check to see if you are experiencing grief or regret about having lived with this limiting belief.

This belief created your life experiences and influenced choices you made. Realizing how this limiting belief influenced your life can bring up feelings of grief, regret, upset, sadness, and anger. Allow yourself to feel these feelings. Say them out loud and tap on them until the emotional charge they hold eases.

At this point check the emotional rating of your limiting belief again.

If it's 5 or lower, go to tapping on letting go of the limiting belief. If the rating is higher than 5, go to letters A-E. (See page 150.)

Tapping on letting go of the old limiting belief

Step 1: Shifting the limiting belief from being true to not true

Step 2: Letting go of the limiting belief

Step 1: Shifting the limiting belief from being true to not true

Before you let the belief go, make sure that all parts of you agree that it is no longer true.

In this step, you first want to introduce the *possibility* that the limiting belief is actually not true. There are many different sentences you can use. You can think of tapping them as opening the door to a new possibility. A little bit or fully, and all the degrees in between.

Here is what it might look and sound like:

> "I could allow/I can allow/I allow myself to open up to the possibility that this belief is not true anymore."

> "It might be possible that this belief is actually not true (anymore)."

> "Even though this belief was true when I grew up, it does not need to be true for the rest of my life."

Chapter 12 | How to Tap to Disslove Limiting Beliefs

"Even though this belief was true for such a long time, it is possible that it's not true anymore."

"It is possible that this belief is actually not true—it is just the meaning I gave my experience when I was 5 years old."

"Even though this belief was true for how my parents treated me, I have many people in my life now who are different from my parents. It is possible that this belief is not true anymore."

"What if this belief is actually not true anymore?"

"I wonder how I would feel if this belief were not true anymore?"

It is important that you find words and sentences that resonate with *you*. The statements need *to feel right* to you. You want to open the door to the possibility that this belief is not true, but don't open the door so wide that you don't believe it.

- When you *feel* the possibility and *sense* a response of openness and excitement in you, you have found the right wording.

- If you are getting bored with the sentence you are using, you might want to open the door a bit more. Use words that are more direct.

- If you feel resistance or you are getting scared, you have opened the door too wide. Choose words that are gentler.

If you sense a hesitation, a holding back from allowing that the old limiting belief is not true anymore, then there is still something in you that wants to be heard, seen, understood, or validated relating to the past traumatic experience you went through. You might notice this as a heaviness, constriction, tension, resistance, or even fear when you say the statements of this new possibility.

Then go to one or more of the areas below and do more tapping rounds.

A. Maybe there is another aspect of the experience/situation of how and when the belief was formed that wants to be addressed—for example, your unmet needs at the time. Maybe you also had a concern about someone else, a sibling, friend, parent, grandparent.

B. Maybe you still need to give yourself more empathy, compassion, understanding, and kindness for how you learned this belief growing up.

C. Maybe there is still a feeling that has not been expressed or validated enough. It could be sadness, anger, terror, frustration, hate, desperation, fear, or loneliness. Sometimes we hold back from allowing feelings that are labelled as "bad" to come to the surface and into our awareness.

D. Maybe you just need to go a little slower and allow time for the emotional and energetic shifts in your body to settle into new places.

E. Maybe there is *another* limiting belief that does not allow *this* limiting belief you are tapping on to shift. The other limiting belief will try to tell you that there is a negative consequence if this old belief would not be true anymore. For example, "If I allow this belief to shift then I would be able to speak up for myself. But if I were to speak up for myself, I would lose my job, or the relationship with my friend, partner, or family would end." Or "I don't know who I would be without this belief. I can't let it go."

Tap on experiences, feelings, body sensations, thoughts, and beliefs you've selected from A to E. Make sure you are coming from empathy, kindness, and acceptance for yourself while you tap. Take your time.

CHAPTER 12 | HOW TO TAP TO DISSOLVE LIMITING BELIEFS

Continue addressing the feelings, body sensations, and thoughts that came up in your hesitation until you feel an openness, ease, joy, excitement, or relief when you say, "It's possible that this old limiting belief is actually not true."

Lightness, ease, flow, tingling, openness, joy, and feelings of excitement are signs that your subconscious is in agreement with your statement about this new possibility. They are messages from your subconscious that say, "The old belief is not true anymore!" At this point all parts of you are realizing and knowing that the learned limiting belief is actually not true.

Step 2: Letting go of the limiting belief

Now you can start tapping on statements about letting go of the limiting belief.

Here again it's important to be patient with yourself!

Parts of you might be so ready to let go of that old limiting belief, really wanting to be done with it. It could be your logical mind, aspects of you that don't like to feel uncomfortable feelings, or patterns you have that know how to push through something. But there might be other parts of you—often from the trauma that caused the limiting belief—that still want to be seen, heard, and understood before they too are ready to let go of the old limiting belief. If that is the case, you will sense that there is a hesitation, a wall, a holding back, or a resistance in your body, your feelings, and your energy. It is important to pay attention to that. The parts of you that want the limiting belief gone might readily say words like "I am letting this belief go," but some of the old subconscious programming is not on board with it.

If you sense hesitation in response to your statements about this letting go, go slower and pay attention to your feelings, body sensations, thoughts, or other beliefs that tell you that there will be negative consequences if you let go of this belief.

Read through the list A–E and find what resonates with you. Tap on it.

At some point you will sense a natural readiness for the limiting belief to shift. You will sense a shift in you when all parts of you relating to this belief have received enough attention and empathy, have been seen and heard, and have been felt and understood.

Now you can move on to letting the belief go. Start by tapping sentences like:

"It might be possible that I can let go of this belief."

"It is possible that I could/can let go of this belief."

"I could/can let go of this belief."

When you sense an openness in you—an ease, joy, flow, excitement—you can be more direct in your statements of letting go:

"I wonder how I would feel if I let this old belief go."

"I am ready to let this old learned belief go more and more."

"This belief is actually not true anymore. I am ready to let it go."

"I am letting this old belief go."

When everything in you is in agreement with the statement of letting this limiting belief go, you will sense an opening, a lightness, joy, relief, maybe tears of joy, an expansion, and a sense of empowerment.

Tapping on a new supportive belief

From this openness a new supportive belief can arise. Often it shows up on its own. And it is actually not new. It has always been there. It was covered up and suppressed by the learned, inherited, or absorbed limiting belief. Now that the limiting belief is gone, the true belief can be noticed.

Chapter 12 | How to Tap to Dissolve Limiting Beliefs

And most likely you sense a deep knowing that the belief that has re-emerged is the truth. It's like remembering who you were before the false limiting belief came into your life.

"I am lovable."

"I am worthy."

"I am wanted."

The beliefs that re-emerge, that show up again are the unchanging truth of the nature of your being!

Sometimes you might want to *create* a new supportive belief. Often these beliefs are specific to what you believe you can have, do, or be in your life. These beliefs relate to your work, income, money, relationships, family, friends, and place in the world.

"I can have a fulfilling job."

"I am capable."

"I can be joyful at my workplace, because I am expressing from my heart."

"If I earn . . . dollars per month/year, others will still like me for who I am."

"I can be in a loving relationship, because I am lovable."

"I can have supportive and fun-loving friends."

"I am safe to do what I am passionate about in my life."

After tapping on the new belief—the one that showed up as your inner truth or the one you created for specific aspects of your life—check to make sure all of you is in agreement with it.

If there are still parts of you that are not in alignment with this new supportive belief, you will feel some holding back, hesitation, doubt, contraction, or block. These are signals from your subconscious. The sense of hesitation or holding back can be very subtle. Be very honest with yourself in listening to these subtle messages.

Go back to A–E if necessary. Tap more rounds on what comes up for you.

Remember, your subconscious language of body sensations, feelings, energies, images, and memories has the wisdom to reprogram inner limitations that your linear and logical mind does not have. Again, be patient! The more you pay attention to the subtle messages of your subconscious and tap on them, the easier it will be to complete the process of dissolving your limiting belief and letting in the new.

When you feel ready, check in again.

When all of you is in agreement with the new supportive belief, you will feel joy, openness, flow, excitement, an increased and forward movement of your energy, or a state of calm. These are signals from your subconscious that all of you is in agreement with the stated new belief.

Testing the result

Now imagine the situation in which you used to feel restricted by your limiting belief. Check out how it feels to you now. How would you feel, think, and act in the old situation now coming from your new belief? Can you live the truth of your new belief in the old situation, be free of the old restrictions? If not, go back and tap on what still shows up in you as hesitation.

If you can be with the old situation while living the truth of your new belief, **celebrate!**

You have freed yourself from a limiting belief!

Chapter 12 | How to Tap to Dissolve Limiting Beliefs

When you dissolve a limiting belief, it will change your feelings, thoughts, and body sensations immediately. It will also change your behaviour and the choices you make. The changes in the outer circumstances of your life most likely will take a bit more time. The manifestations on the outside that are bound in time and space don't move as quickly as your feelings, thoughts, and body sensations shift! Don't use this slower change as proof that dissolving your limiting belief didn't work. It needs some communicating and arranging in the different realms of the universe for that new job, or the love or friendships you now allow yourself to have, to show up in your life. Be patient about when and how the effects of the dissolving of your limiting beliefs manifest on the outside. Move into gratitude and love for your new supportive belief and into joyful curiosity and anticipation of what will change in your outside world.

Chapter 13

Examples of Tapping to Dissolve Limiting Beliefs

Let's go through two examples of tapping together. The steps refer to the Tapping Protocol for Dissolving Limiting Beliefs in Appendix 4.

Tapping example 1

For years Peter felt anxious at work. He finally decided to do something about it. Instead of continuing with his same old efforts to cope with his anxiety, he started to be curious about what was causing it. He became aware that he feels especially anxious when he has thoughts of not-being-good-enough, and he realized that he actually has the belief "I am not good enough."

He decided to tap on it.

II. Starting point if you know your limiting belief

1. Name and rate your limiting belief.

Peter names his belief "I am not good enough." Intellectually, he knows he is quite accomplished and one of the most capable employees in the company he works for. But when he tunes into his feeling sense of the belief, he gets the rating number 8. The belief feels very true to him.

2. Create your set-up statement and tap it three times on the karate chop point.

He creates his set-up statement: "Even though I have this belief that I am not good enough, I choose to be gentle and kind to myself."

He taps that statement three times on the karate chop point.

3. Tap on the belief or on feelings, body sensations, thoughts, memories, energies, images—any context that comes up around this belief. Do check-ins after your rounds. Use the information that comes up in your check-ins for your next statements.

Then he moves into tapping a whole round on the belief "I am not good enough." He uses different statements while tapping on that belief: "I am not good enough. I have this belief that I am not good enough. I learned to believe that I am not good enough. Somehow I ended up with this belief that I am not good enough."

At the end of the round he does his check-in, listening to his inner response to the tapping. He notices a tightness in his throat and a knot in his stomach, and that he's also holding his breath a bit.

He taps another round using the information from his check-in: "My throat feels tight. I feel this knot in my stomach. I am holding my breath a bit."

After the round he checks in again. He notices that he feels angry. He taps on that too: "I feel angry. My throat feels tight. I have this knot in my stomach. I feel angry."

Chapter 13 | Examples of Tapping to Dissolve Limiting Beliefs

After this round he checks in again, and he remembers how his dad used to correct him a lot.

Then all of a sudden, he remembers and shares: "My dad always knew better. It seemed there was always something I didn't do quite right. I hated that."

4. Tap on how this belief came into your life.

a. Through making meaning of experiences growing up

"I remember I built this little shelf once. It was spring break. I must have been 8. I felt so good about it. I wanted to put my rock collection on it, and it was really fun. And then my dad came home from work and saw me in the workshop with the shelf almost finished. He said that the boards didn't quite line up, and which saw was I using? That next time I should use the other one. And that nails were poking out. The nails were too long, and I needed to measure the thickness of the boards and then choose the right size nails." He looks down at the floor.

"All of a sudden, the joy I'd had building that little shelf was gone. I'd thought my dad would be proud of me having built that little shelf by myself, but he wasn't. I had this sense that I wasn't good enough." He pauses.

"Wow, I hadn't thought about this for so long."

After Peter remembers and shares this experience, he taps on it. One sentence per tapping point, using several rounds to do it.

Afterward, he takes a deep breath into his belly and a long slow breath out. He checks in with what he notices. "I feel a bit lighter. My shoulders are usually very tight. I feel they are more relaxed now. The knot in my stomach is gone."

b. Through absorbing and/or inheriting the belief growing up

Peter realizes, "My dad had very high standards and expectations of himself all the time. He grew up in Holland. Grandpa always wanted his sons to do really well. And my dad did so much. He always worked and did more than other people I know."

The question of whether Peter thinks his dad has the same limiting belief of not-being-good-enough comes up.

"I've never thought of it, but that makes so much sense. Yes, I think he has the same belief. He always needs to prove and show how much he does and how well he does things. Maybe he has to convince himself that he is good enough, and also prove it to others."

Peter does some tapping on these realizations. "This belief that I am not good enough—my dad has the same belief. Maybe even my grandpa had this belief. We are actually very capable men. We can't and couldn't really enjoy our achievements because of this belief of not being good enough."

5. Tap on possible grief, regret, anger, sadness about having acquired and lived with this belief—the effect this belief has had on your life.

In his check-in Peter notices that "The tightness, constriction in my throat is still there. I somehow feel sad."

He does another round of tapping. He taps on being sad. "I am sad that my dad wasn't proud of me. I am sad that the joy building the little shelf was gone. I am sad that it wasn't fun doing something with my dad. I am sad that my dad couldn't connect with me in the joy of doing things, that it was always about doing it right and well. I am really sad that I haven't been able to enjoy all my achievements. There was always this burden of not

Chapter 13 | Examples of Tapping to Dissolve Limiting Beliefs

being good enough. I am really sad about it. So many unhappy years."

Peter tears up and continues to tap. "I am really sad about all those years I felt that burden. I always felt so anxious at work, wondering if my boss was going to tell me that my project was not progressing fast enough or that I had done something wrong. I always felt so anxious. So sad that it took the joy out of my work."

6. Rate your belief again.

Peter does a check-in. He notices that the tightness in his throat is gone. He feels tired but also relieved. He rates his belief "I am not good enough." It is now a 4.

7. Tap on shifting the belief from being true to not true.

Peter is now ready to tap on shifting the belief from being true to not true. He uses several different statements for it. "Maybe it is possible that the belief 'I am not good enough' is not true. It actually might be possible that this belief is not true. What if this belief is actually not true? I could allow myself to believe that it is not true."

He does another check-in. He feels less tired. He also notices that there is a bit of a hesitation in him to fully say that this belief is not true.

We talk about the old parenting style where parents thought that if they told their kids what they were doing wrong, the kids would do better. It would help them to succeed in life. Most often this way of parenting was well intentioned. Back then there was no one who could show parents better ways to support their child to be successful. And there was no one who could tell the child that their parents were actually proud of them but simply did not know how to express it.

A and B

Peter taps on this: "Maybe that my dad didn't say that he is proud of me didn't have anything to do with me, but with the way *he* grew up. Maybe what I did was actually really good for my age back then. Maybe my dad actually saw that, but he couldn't say that he was proud of me."

He tears up.

During his check-in he realizes how much he always longed for his dad to see and appreciate him as he figured things out for himself. He also wanted him to notice how much fun he had. Peter thought again that his dad was always focused on doing things right and well. That enjoying doing things was not important to him.

He taps again: "I am so sad that my dad couldn't see my joy and excitement building that little shelf back then. I am so sad that my dad couldn't see that I actually was so proud of myself. I am sad that my dad couldn't connect with me in the joy of doing things, that it was always about doing it right and well. I always hoped my dad wouldn't be so serious about things."

During his check-in Peter notices that he feels a relief.

He taps again on the belief not being true, and this time the hesitation he felt earlier is gone.

8. Tap on letting the limiting belief go.

Peter is now ready to let the old belief go. He taps these statements: "I could let this belief go. I wonder how it would feel if I let this belief go. I can choose to let this belief go more and more. I am so done with this old belief. I choose to let it go now."

He does a check-in. He feels lighter and happier. He feels hopeful.

9. Tap on the supportive new belief.

Peter is ready to tap on the new belief.

"I could allow myself to believe that I am good enough. I can allow myself to know that I am good enough. I can trust more and more that I am good enough. What if I am actually good enough?" He laughs. "I *am* actually good enough. I realize that it was a passed-down belief from the male side of my family. We are all actually good enough."

He takes a moment, and in his mind and heart he sends acknowledgement and the new belief of being good enough to his dad, his grandfather, and his great-grandfather, and all the fathers who came before them.

He taps this: "I am good enough. I know now that I am good enough. Actually, I always was good enough. And I know that my dad, my granddad, and my great-granddad were always good enough."

10. Test the result.

Now Peter imagines being at work the following week with this new belief of being good enough. He sees himself walk into his office with relaxed shoulders and a smile on his face. He feels excited.

Tapping example 2

Katie is very upset about a rift that had developed between her close friend and her. She has been thinking about this a lot and has felt many different emotions come up without finding a resolution for the situation with her friend or peace within herself. She feels hurt and heartbroken that her friend was not interested in listening and being there for her feelings and experiences. Katie does not know yet which limiting belief connects to her experience with her friend.

I. Starting point if you don't know your limiting belief

1. Create a statement about your feelings, your body sensations, your thoughts, a situation, a trigger, an unfulfilled need, dream, or goal.

Katie decides to start with the heartbreak she is feeling. She creates her first statement: "I feel so heartbroken about this close friendship."

2. Create your set-up statement and tap it three times on the karate chop point.

She creates her set-up statement: "Even though I feel so heartbroken about this close friendship, I choose to be compassionate and loving with myself."

She taps that statement three times on the karate chop point.

3. Continue tapping rounds on points 2–9 using statements of feelings, experiences, body sensations, thoughts, memories of situations, unfulfilled needs, dreams, or goals.

Katie continues tapping a round using these sentences: "I feel so heartbroken. I am sad and upset that she was not interested in my experience. I also feel angry."

4. Do check-ins after each round. Continue tapping on the statement you started with or use statements that hold the information from your check-ins.

During her check-in Katie notices thoughts about her brother and sister and that they also don't really listen to her when she shares her feelings and experiences. She feels hurt by that.

She taps: "My siblings are not really interested in my experiences. They don't really listen to me sharing my feelings. I feel hurt by that."

She does another check-in and notices a memory coming up. "I remember sitting on the edge of the lawn. I was 5 years old. My brother and sister and our neighbourhood friends were playing. They didn't invite me in, and I didn't feel included. I thought they didn't want to be with me because I have my feelings and opinions."

Katie taps a round on that memory one sentence at a time.

5. Do the tapping while holding curiosity about your underlying belief. When you are ready, ask yourself, "What must I believe that I feel/sense/think/experience this?"

During her check-in Katie realizes that she often has this thought that others don't want to be with her. She notices that these thoughts are actually a belief she has: "Others don't want to be with me because of my feelings and opinions."

We talk about how we formed beliefs as little children, giving meaning to our experiences from the limited life experience we've had at that point. And that everything around us also had meaning about us because we were in a state of connectedness.

Katie now moves on to tapping on her limiting belief.

II. Starting point if you know your limiting belief

1. Name and rate your limiting belief.

Katie names her belief and rates it. This belief, "Others don't want to be with me because of my feelings and opinions," feels like a 7 or 8.

Then she goes right to step 4a.

4. Tap on how this belief came into your life.

a. Through making meaning of experiences growing up

Katie taps: "I tried to find an explanation for why the other kids didn't invite me in. And I thought they didn't want to be with me because of my feelings and opinions. But actually, maybe the other kids were just engaged in their play and didn't think of inviting me. Maybe they would have been totally ok with me joining in."

3. Tap on the belief or on feelings, body sensations, thoughts, memories, energies, images—any context that comes up around this belief. Do check-ins after your rounds. Use the information that comes up in your check-ins for your next statements.

During her check-in Katie remembers, "My mom often said 'Shush' when we were in public, so we wouldn't be too loud. I thought, I am too much."

She also remembers other situations with kids, where she believed they thought she was weird or not good enough.

Katie taps on these memories one sentence at a time. She sometimes repeats one of them until the emotional charge they hold lessens: "I remember my mom saying 'Shush' when we were in

Chapter 13 | Examples of Tapping to Dissolve Limiting Beliefs

public. She didn't want us to be so loud. I thought that I am too much. Later, I often had this feeling that I am too much for others."

And: "I remember situations with other kids, where I thought, 'They think that I am weird or that I am not good enough.' I somehow didn't feel included."

Katie also remembers many friendships in the past where she felt rejected. Where others were not interested in what she felt and experienced. She taps on these memories as well.

5. Tap on possible grief, regret, anger, sadness about having acquired and lived with this belief—the effect this belief has had on your life.

We talk about how our beliefs unconsciously inform others how to behave around us. That we also unconsciously choose people to begin with who have a tendency to behave according to our beliefs. And when others behave in alignment with what we believe, we use that in return to confirm those beliefs.

Katie finds that she's actually experiencing now that people who are new in her life are curious about her. That they are valuing her for who she is. She taps a round on that.

She realizes that she has missed a lot of opportunities with others because of this old belief that others don't want to be with her.

She taps on it: "I am sad that because of this old belief I missed so many opportunities with others. I am really upset about it. I could choose to hold myself in gentleness. I choose to hold myself in compassion and forgiveness for it."

6. Rate your belief again.

Katie rates her belief again. It is now a 4.

7. Tap on shifting the belief from being true to not true.

Katie taps, "What if this belief 'Others don't want to be with me' is actually not true? What if it was just a misinterpretation of me as a 5-year-old? I didn't know any better. It might actually not be true. What if it was never really true?" Katie taps several rounds using these statements.

She rates her belief again and it is now a 2.

8. Tap on letting the limiting belief go.

Katie taps rounds on letting go of this limiting belief: "What if I could let this belief go a bit? What if I don't have to hold it for the rest of my life? Maybe I don't have to have this belief anymore. I wonder how my body would feel if I didn't have this belief anymore. I can choose to let this belief go more and more. I wonder how my life would be without this belief."

Katie shared that at some point when tapping these rounds she had a sense that the belief went out the top of her head.

9. Tap on the supportive new belief.

Katie taps on introducing a new supportive belief: "What if others would want to be with me? What if they are actually interested in my feelings, my experiences, in me? I could choose to allow that others want to be with me. I could allow that others are interested in being with me. I can allow that others want to be with me. What if I could enjoy others being interested in me?"

During her check-in Katie notices that "I feel more space, more self-love. I also have more compassion for these stories and patterns in myself and others."

CHAPTER 13 | EXAMPLES OF TAPPING TO DISSOLVE LIMITING BELIEFS

9. Test the result.

Katie imagines being with friends. She notices that part of her fears that old thoughts and doubts might show up again. She decides to be really aware when that happens and to choose questions like:

"What if this old thought is actually not true anymore?"

"What if others do want to be with me?"

You might have noticed that Katie had formed variations of the belief "Others don't want to be with me":

"Others don't want to be with me because of my feelings and my opinions."

"Others don't want to be with me because I am too much."

"Others don't want to be with me because they think I am weird."

"Others don't want to be with me because I am not good enough."

Each one of these beliefs needs to be tapped on. It can be done in one or several sessions, depending on time and energy, and on what comes up relating to each variation.

In this tapping sequence, Katie focused on "Others don't want to be with me because of my feelings and opinions." When she imagined being with friends, she noticed that there were still fears of old thoughts coming up. It could very well be that this was fuelled by the variations of her belief that still needed to be tapped on.

Chapter 14

Dos and Don'ts for Tapping

What actually happens when you tap to dissolve a limiting belief?

1. You get the amygdala out of alarm mode and, by doing so, the brain and body into a calmer state.

2. You dissolve negative associations and limiting beliefs you formed through past experiences.

3. You create—and allow to surface—new associations and beliefs that are life-enhancing and life-supporting.

In order to move through and complete these three steps you need to follow certain dos and don'ts in your tapping process of dissolving a limiting belief.

You might find this summary especially helpful if you get stuck in your tapping process. Most likely it will help you to create a flow in your tapping again. (Note that we covered some of these points in earlier chapters.)

- The linear mind cannot change the program of the nonlinear, subconscious mind—but it can be very helpful in reminding you to tap! **Do** let the linear mind remind you to tap and to use all the information you have about the tapping process.

- **Don't** try to get rid of the "unwanted," challenging pattern, belief, habit, feeling, or situation that you are tapping on. Don't push against it. Thoughts like "I want this to go away" or "I want to fix this, and I know that tapping works" undermine the effectiveness of your tapping process.

- **Do** move into acceptance. You do that in your set-up statement. For example, "Even though I have this belief of not being good enough, I choose to be gentle and kind with myself." You create space between that "unwanted" experience or belief and yourself. You create detachment from what you want to change. And by doing so, what you want to change can go on its journey of unravelling back to what is true.

- **Don't** try to figure things out intellectually while you are tapping.

- **Do** allow your subconscious to take the lead. In our Western culture we approach many things with a linear goal and approach. Using that here blocks the magic of tapping. When you tap, allow yourself to not know and to trust that something good will come out of your tapping sequence.

I have seen so many amazing changes guiding my clients through tapping sequences. Over and over I am touched by the magic that happens when we allow ourselves to follow our inner wisdom and the signals of our subconscious knowing.

- **Do** tap on what is present for you in the moment. Sometimes when you have a specific idea about what you want to tap on, something else that you are sensing, feeling, or thinking can dominate your awareness. When this happens, let go of your plan and instead tap on the feelings, thoughts, body sensations, and memories that you are aware of right now. It might

Chapter 14 | Dos and Don'ts for Tapping

even lead you to what you wanted to tap on to begin with. If it doesn't, you can go back to the issue later. Trust the process.

- **Do** let go of wanting a specific outcome. This is part of trusting the unknown. When you start your tapping sequence you can set an intention for an inner shift, but don't be too specific about the outcome.

- **Do** use words that feel true to you. Find exactly the right words for *you*. Your words and your statements need to resonate with you for them to be effective in your tapping. Adapt your sentences to achieve that.

- **Don't** use words and sentences that are complicated or complex. Sentences with conceptual and complex content come from the linear, logical, and conceptual mind. They are connected to the beta brainwave state. They can't communicate with your subconscious belief programs.

- **Do** use the language of the alpha and theta brainwave state, the language of the subconscious. This language uses words of feelings, body sensations, images, and energies. Sentences that keep the magic of tapping alive are short, simple, and feeling-focused.

- Sometimes, when your emotions are strong, you might have swear words come up. **Do** use these for tapping. It's okay. Sometimes you might also want to talk directly to someone in your tapping. **Do** address them directly even though they are not present. For example, "I am so mad at you for what you did."

- Sometimes what you are tapping on is strongly related to a particular age when you were young. **Do** use words you would have used as the 3-, 4-, 5-, 6-, or 7-year-old you. If you are tapping on experiences from a time when you were even younger and you didn't have words yet, **do** use words you would say as a caring, loving, and protective adult for the young you. Name the feelings, body sensations, and experiences for the baby or toddler you once were.

- **Do** *feel* what you are tapping. Use words and statements that are alive and/or charged for you.

- **Do** keep tapping. Very occasionally you might experience that your feelings are so strong for a moment that you can't speak. If this happens, keep tapping on the points without saying anything. It usually takes only a few points of tapping for the feelings to be less intense and for your voice to come back. Trust your process.

- **Do** open the door to change just the right amount by using phrases like "I could, I can, I can learn, a little bit, more and more, it might be, it could be, it might be possible . . . "

- **Do** use compassion and curiosity in your tapping. During your tapping, have part of you hold yourself in compassion while another part is doing all the feeling and experiencing of the tapping statements. Be gently curious about your experiences of how the limiting belief came into your life and influenced it.

- **Do** change your tapping statements if you notice self-judgment. Sometimes you might notice that you are judging yourself for the experiences, feelings, thoughts, or beliefs you are tapping on. If this happens, stop what you are tapping on and tap on your judgment instead. It will take you on another little journey and show you your beliefs that created that judgment.

Chapter 14 | Dos and Don'ts for Tapping

- **Do** allow enough space, time, and energy for your tapping.

- **Don't** tap on big issues—limiting beliefs—when you are tired or you only have a few minutes.

- **Do** interrupt and close your tapping if necessary. It might be that you run out of time, private space, or energy. It might be that you feel uncomfortable with or overwhelmed by what is coming up emotionally. Put your experience in a sentence and tap it. End with tapping a sentence that states the closing of your tapping for now.

- **Do** hold yourself and what you are tapping on in acceptance and compassion.

- **Do** let the tapping process unfold step by step.

- **Do** bring your awareness to your connection with the ground.

- **Do** remember that we are all in this together.

Most importantly,

Do hold yourself in gentleness!

Chapter 15

When a Recommended Action Promises to Fulfill Your Goals and Dreams

In our Western culture most of us focus a lot on strategies and actions and less on our needs, feelings, and the underlying beliefs. So it is not surprising that you often hear or read about people sharing that they used a specific strategy and it created a desired outcome. This specific action, the strategy, might then be recommended as *the* way for others to achieve their goals and dreams as well.

> *It is not the action or strategy that determines the outcome, but the belief, motivation, agenda, and energy underlying the action or strategy...*
> *When actions or strategies are backed by supportive beliefs, they will help you to achieve your goals and dreams!*

When you read or hear about such actions and strategies you might get very excited. Maybe you think as we often do, "Now I have found what I need to do to reach my goal!" You feel motivated, hopeful, inspired, and energized to use that specific strategy to reach your goal—until your limiting beliefs pull you back.

The actions or strategies themselves do not determine whether or not you reach your goal. What *is* important in determining success is how these actions and strategies relate to your beliefs!

When actions and strategies are backed by supportive beliefs, there is a good chance you'll achieve your desired outcome and reach your goals. When your actions and strategies are not backed by your beliefs, they are not going to work.

Let's look at some examples.

- Example 1: The action of giving to others is often recommended as a way to achieve happiness. For thousands of years women's role was to give to others, care for others, and nurture others, often at the expense of their own well-being, receiving, and truest self-expression. Conditioning and beliefs formed around these experiences. These old traditional roles are changing now. The younger generations are holding more balanced patterns of masculine and feminine energy. But even though these roles and energies are changing, many women still hold beliefs like:

"I have to give to others."

"I am not worthy to receive without giving more to others."

"I have to attend to the needs of others first before attending to my own needs."

"The needs of others are more important than mine."

If a person with beliefs like these tries to achieve happiness by giving to others, the giving will come from the old limiting belief and not from joy. The giving will actually confirm their old limiting belief and keep them excluded from giving and receiving freely. It will most likely not bring them the happiness they seek.

- Example 2: A man starts a diet that promises a weight loss of a certain number of pounds per week. He is very motivated to lose those pounds. The weight loss goes really well for the first three weeks. Then he starts to move away from the diet and regains all the pounds. He might have beliefs like:

"I need to have my weight around me to feel safe with others."

"I don't deserve to have a fit and healthy body."

"If I had less body weight, I would have to live my life dreams. I am afraid of failing them."

It will be those beliefs, not the prescribed strategy for the promised weight loss, that prove to be true.

Belief versus strategy

It is not the action or strategy that determines the outcome, but the belief, motivation, agenda, and energy underlying the action or strategy.

So, if you hear or read that you should take a specific action or follow a specific strategy to achieve a certain outcome regarding your:

- weight,
- exercise routine,
- health,
- well-being,
- relationships,
- work,
- finances,

- happiness, or
- spirituality,

pay attention to your beliefs, your motivation, your agenda, and the energy you use in doing so.

You might be very excited at first about following the recommended action or strategy, but after a while you might give up and stop focusing on your goal. If this is a pattern you experience frequently, become curious about your limiting beliefs that will always pull you back to *their* truth. When you find your limiting belief, dissolve it and change it to a supportive one. *Then* use the recommended action or strategy or other strategies that you'd like to try.

When actions or strategies are backed by supportive beliefs, they will help you to achieve your goals and dreams!

Chapter 16

Our Invisible Websites

You know how you sometimes "get" information about others without them doing or saying anything? With people you know, you might feel their moods as soon as you enter the house, before you even see them. And with strangers you might sense something about them without even talking to them.

You can somehow sense a lot about people, including:

- whether they like themselves or not,
- whether they feel loved by others or not, and
- whether they believe they can do things in their lives they are passionate about or not.

How is this possible?

Our thoughts, feelings, and beliefs are vibrating energy. The unseen vibrational patterns and forms of our thoughts, feelings, and beliefs exist as energetic information in and around our physical body. It's as if we have a "personal website" with all our information on it being broadcast to the world.

You can imagine this website with menu items comprising your character traits and your beliefs. There are posts that change frequently, like your feelings and thoughts. And there are blogs with your stories. Without any electronic devices, others can "read" your invisible website—and you can "read" theirs. As human beings we have done this forever, mostly without being aware of it.

Our patterns and beliefs from all their different sources are part of the content of our invisible websites.

Your "website" with your energetic information communicates with the "website" of others constantly—so much for privacy! This is how you are attracted to one person and not to another. Something on their website connects with something on yours, through either similarity or contrast.

- You might be attracted to a person whose passions or energies are similar to yours. You easily create joyful experiences together.

- Or the two of you might have complementary patterns and beliefs on your websites—perhaps you have the belief "I need others to take care of me," and so you attract someone with the menu item "I have to take care of others in order to be loved," or vice versa.

- The same is true for the menu item "My needs don't matter." If that is on the dropdown menu of your invisible website, someone might subconsciously and energetically respond with "I can confirm that for you." That person then mirrors your limiting belief by behaving and talking in ways that show that your needs don't matter.

- Luckily it works in the same way for supportive beliefs like "I am lovable." If that is on the dropdown menu of your invisible website, others might subconsciously and energetically mirror that supportive belief by behaving and talking in ways that are loving toward you.

- In addition, you might also experience a resistance to information on someone's website. You might notice it as judgment, negative feelings, or a sense of you pulling back energetically.

These patterns that attract, complement, or resist each other might look like this:

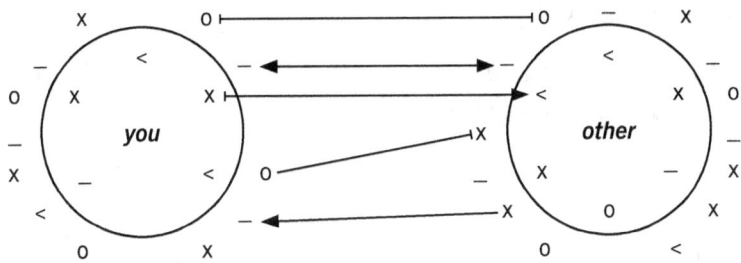

- x patterns/beliefs from experiences in childhood
- < patterns/beliefs taken on from parents, inherited from ancestors
- — patterns/beliefs from society/culture/church
- o patterns/beliefs from past lives

When your "website communications" with others happen unconsciously, you don't have much choice. You react to their feelings, thoughts, stories, and beliefs without consciously choosing to do so. And you feel powerless when others react to yours.

When you are aware of your own and the other person's thoughts, feelings, patterns, and beliefs, you are empowered. And you have a choice about how you want to be. You can move from automatic reactions to consciously choosing how you want to think, feel, and behave.

Then you stop seeing your invisible website and the invisible websites of others as truth and instead you see them as something that was created, mostly unconsciously. It's just like websites you access on your computer, phone, or tablet. You don't think of them as truth but as information that was created and posted by someone.

PART II | DISSOLVING YOUR LIMITING BELIEFS

The more conscious you are of the content of your own invisible website the more you can decide which menu items, posts, and blogs you want to keep, change, or delete. You can take ownership of it and take control over what is posted.

The moment you change what is on your invisible website, something else will change:

- Others will respond to the changes by behaving differently toward and around you.
- New and different people might be attracted to your website.
- Others might lose interest in your invisible website. They will move more into the background, or even out of your life because the content of your website does not sync with the content of theirs anymore.

A gift you can give someone is to not interpret what's on their invisible website as truth. You could instead choose to hold the other person in compassion in their limiting beliefs and choose to see and know them as their true being. To be able to do this, you need to know yourself as your true being and really become conscious of your own invisible website.

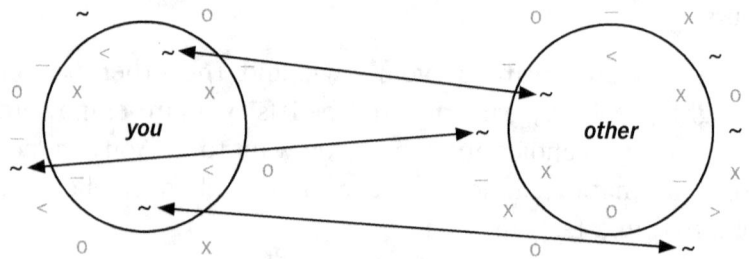

~ **vibration of Highest Consciousness, the energy of true being**

The most profound change you can make on your invisible website is to update your beliefs!

Chapter 17

How to Ask for What You Want from Abundance Instead of Scarcity

In our Western societies, we have a history and heritage of scarcity thinking. For many centuries, and many, many generations, the focus has been on what was missing, what was wrong, and what needed improving and fixing. And that way of thinking and operating has contributed to an immense improvement in many areas of our collective lives.

This approach does not work very well, though, when we apply it to people. When we focus on our lack and others' lack, on what is wrong with us and them, on our and their not-good-enoughness. And when we focus on what needs to be fixed in ourselves and others, the energy in us shifts. What happens on the deepest level in those moments of focusing on lack and what's "wrong" is that we disconnect from The Divine in us and in the other.

This disconnect when we think of scarcity and wrongness shows up as judging ourselves and others. It creates feelings and experiences of unmet needs. It can show up as sadness, depression, and constricted energy. As anger, frustration, disappointment. As the felt sense of a block, a wall, a barrier. As a sense of not being seen, of somehow being flawed.

Or we might create a boosted sense of being "better than" if we project the wrongness onto others. In our hearts we know it is fake. The list of experiences of unmet needs related to this disconnect seem endless.

The urge to "improve," to "fix," or to "heal" this wrongness, lack, not-good-enoughness is not motivated by joy and inspiration. When you tell yourself, "I am lacking in . . . ," "Something is wrong with me," or "I need to fix, heal, improve this . . . in me," or when you think, "The other is wrong/bad and needs to be fixed," there is no joy, ease, love, or flow.

We can always learn more, improve, and expand. It is our innate nature to do so. When the learning, improving, and expansion is coming from joy, love, curiosity, giving, caring, and excitement, then you are in true connection with yourself and others.

But most of us come from generations and generations of pointing out lack, wrongness, failure, and not-good-enoughness, and of patterns of criticism of self and others. This criticism was and still is used as a means to make ourselves and the other person "better." It is connected to the false belief that if I stopped criticizing myself or other people, there would be no growing, learning, changing, or improving.

And even though this kind of criticism might have led to better grades at school, better table manners, or polite behaviours in children, it did not create "better" people. On the contrary, it contributed greatly to the perpetuation of the limiting beliefs we hold about ourselves personally and share collectively. The beliefs about being wrong, bad, not good enough, not worthy, and not deserving. When we focus on what is missing and lacking, we miss noticing the inherent goodness in ourselves and others.

We forget that the driving force for that kind of thinking is always our own need!

- A parent who criticizes their child for an emotional outburst in public might be afraid of others criticizing them as a parent. They might have a need to be accepted.

- A person who sees lack, fault, or wrongness in their partner might have a need for support, love, and being cared for.

- A parent who sees deficiency in their child's academic performance might have a need for success for their child—ultimately the need to be a successful parent.

- A person who criticizes a friend for being slow to respond to text messages might have a need for connection and closeness.

In both our personal lives and humanity collectively, we are in a transition period of changing this old pattern. It can be seen in parenting, relationships, business models, work situations, and education. More and more the focus is on the well-being of people and less on finding fault and scarcity. For example:

- In parenting, a child who has a temper tantrum in public might be held firmly and lovingly by their parent and met with understanding for their upset and unmet needs.

- In business and work situations, a staff member whose performance is dropping might be asked how they are doing and what is going on in their life and be offered support.

- In education, a child who has difficulty reading and writing might not be called stupid anymore but have their intelligence acknowledged. Perhaps they would be supported by specific ways of learning that met their learning style.

One shift *you* can make in your own life to contribute to this change is in how you ask for something. You can shift your asking for what you want from others by coming from a sense of abundance instead of lack.

Let's explore that shift in more detail.

The old way: Communicating from lack

Imagine you come home from work. You are tired. Your partner is watching TV. The kitchen is a mess. You feel frustrated, upset, somewhat angry.

You find fault in your partner. You might say, "Can't you clean the kitchen before you watch TV? I work all day, and then I come home, and the kitchen is a mess." Your partner gets reactive and defensive and responds, "You're not the only one working. I deserve a break."

The new way: Communicating from abundance

Even though most of the time we think of communicating as *saying* something to another person, there is actually always an inner communication that happens before we do that. With this new way, we want to pay close attention to this inner communication and shift it to a place of abundance.

Your inner communication

You remember your intention about asking for what you want from abundance.

You notice your feelings and you remember that unhappy feelings—frustration, upset, and anger—signal unmet needs.

You identify your needs instead of going for a strategy. You pause and check in with yourself: "What is my need right now?" You realize that wanting a clean kitchen is actually a strategy and not your need.

You notice that what you really need is some empathy because you are tired from your day at work. You want to rest and relax and feel close to your partner.

You imagine and feel your needs being fulfilled. You can use the powerful questions that we will cover in chapter 18, The Power of "What If . . ." and How to Ask Questions That Move You Forward, to help you *feel* these needs being fulfilled. You can ask, for example, "How would I feel right now if my needs for empathy, closeness, warmth, and relaxation were all fulfilled?"

You allow yourself to feel that and might notice that you relax and soften a bit. You might notice that you are taking deeper breaths. You might sense that you have a smile on your face and feel your heart opening.

When you can hold the thoughts of your needs being fulfilled and feel the body sensations and feelings this creates within you, *then* you are ready for your outer communication.

Your outer communication

Communicate your needs from your inner abundance. Then you can say to your partner, "I am so tired from work. I just need to rest and relax for a while. Could you hold me for a bit? Being held by you makes me feel close to you. It would help me to take deep breaths again and relax." Then you might notice that the mess in the kitchen does not matter anymore.

Or you might notice that it is still important. If so, you could say, "Knowing that the kitchen still needs to be cleaned makes it hard for me to relax, and I feel so tired. Would you clean it before dinner?"

And your partner might say, "How about I make you a cup of tea. And while you have your tea, I'll clean up the kitchen. And then we can decide if we want to order some food in or cook something here."

It sounds ideal, doesn't it?

It makes so much sense to communicate like this instead of the old way of seeing fault, wrongness, and lack.

Going through the steps above and practising them in your mind, heart, and body will improve your ability to communicate in this new way. The really important part to remember is this: When you see fault, wrongness, and lack in yourself, others, or the situation, **there is a need in you that wants to be met!**

What is crucial in this process is to take enough time for the **inner communication**! We often think communicating means saying things out loud. But the most important part of communicating well is the communication within yourself *before you even speak*. Usually we do that part really quickly by unconsciously confirming old patterns, thoughts, and beliefs within ourselves. Then we rush into our outer communication just as unconsciously.

> *Even though most of the time we think of communicating as saying something to another person, there is actually always an inner communication that happens before we do that. It is important to pay close attention to this inner communication and shift it to a place of abundance.*

With this new way of communicating, you want to **consciously** choose your thoughts and feelings about your needs and then move into imagining abundance. The moment you ask from inner fullness, you already feel that you have what you want and need. The likelihood of the other person being open to giving you what you want and need is then way higher. But even if the other person does not give you what you are asking for in that moment, it does not take away from your inner fullness. You are okay with a "no" or a "not right now" from them. There is no judgment of the other, yourself, or the situation. You are also more likely to appreciate the needs of others. And you trust that you can find a different strategy to fulfill your need in your outer experience.

What can be a stumbling block in this way of communicating from fulfillment and abundance is—you guessed it—your limiting beliefs!

Your outer communication is 95 percent nonverbal and only 5 percent verbal. That means most of your communication signals have nothing to do with the words you say!

What shows up in your nonverbal communication is what's really going on inside you. Your thoughts, your feelings, and your relationship to your needs are deeply influenced by your beliefs, and these are communicated by you nonverbally! So, do take time for your inner communication. Become aware of your beliefs about your feelings and needs.

If, despite your practising asking from abundance, things aren't flowing and the other person frequently reacts in a negative or reactive way, be curious about what beliefs are blocking the fulfillment of your needs. It could be, for example, "My needs don't matter." "My needs are not important." "I am not important." "Others don't listen to me." "Others don't support me." Such beliefs make it harder to feel and imagine the fulfillment of your needs. And even though you use the right words in your outer communication, the tone of your voice and the energy of your message will let your limiting beliefs shine through. The other person reacts to this nonverbal communication!

Find out where your beliefs are aligned and not aligned with what you would like to ask for. Then align them as much as possible with the fulfillment of your needs. Most of the time this cannot be done in a few minutes. Use the steps outlined in chapters 12, How to Tap to Dissolve Limiting Beliefs, and 13, Examples of Tapping to Dissolve Limiting Beliefs, for dissolving these limiting beliefs. Allow yourself time for this process. The more you have your beliefs aligned with what you want to ask for, the easier it will be for you to imagine and feel the fulfillment of your needs *before you speak*.

Be patient with yourself. It takes practice, practice, and more practice. It's like learning a new language. You know how awkward it feels to speak in a foreign language when you are new at it? It's the same here. It might feel strange and unfamiliar to take so much time for your inner communication. And it might feel awkward and a bit uncomfortable at first to choose different words for your outer communication. But when you see that it works so much better than the old way, something in you will want to do it more and more often.

Chapter 18

The Power of "What If..." and How to Ask Questions That Move You Forward

Remember when you played as a child and you said, "What if I'm a captain? And what if this is our ship?" And your friend said, "Yes, and what if I'm the person who climbs up the mast?" And then, "What if there's another ship coming?" And off you went—imagining, playing, feeling, being, interacting... You created your own world and it was powerful. You felt alive and present in it. The words "What if..." that were fuelling your imagination turned into "I am..." It was no longer "*What if* I'm the captain of this ship?" but "*I am* the captain of this ship." You *were* the captain and you *were* on a ship. And your friend *was* on the mast, *seeing* another ship coming.

Then you learned another way to use "What if..." You learned to think and say:

"What if something bad happens?"

"What if the other kids don't like me?"

"What if the other kids think I am stupid?"

"What if there is a monster in the closet?"

You learned *this* "What if..." from your experiences and from the people around you who came from a history of trauma. It was fuelled by fear and memories of hurt, pain, and a sense of not being safe. *This* "What if . . . " was something you actually didn't want to happen.

Now that you are an adult you use both forms of "What if . . . "

- The first one moves you toward your dreams.
- The second one keeps you connected to trauma and fear. It keeps you stuck. It keeps your worries alive. It feeds your fear and anxiety.

What if you could use the power of "What if . . . " to feel what you want to feel, to experience what you want to experience, and to create what you want to create?! Just like when you were playing as a child.

AND you can use it to dissolve your limiting beliefs!

Let's look at what happens when you use a "What if . . . " question to dissolve a limiting belief.

Let's take the belief "I am not good enough"—or a variation like "I am not good enough to deserve to be happy" or "I have to be/do/have . . . in order to be good enough."

You can say to yourself, "What if this belief is actually not true? What if I *am* good enough?" You open the door to a new possibility. You engage your mind, body, heart, and soul in feeling, sensing, seeing, thinking, and experiencing *that* possibility!

You are **not** saying, "I am good enough."

You **are** saying, "*What if* I am goosd enough?"

It's like an invitation to what could be. It is important to be with the possibility and potentiality of that change. When you shift too quickly from the belief "I am not good enough" to its opposite belief—"I am good enough"—your subconscious program will go into resistance. All the information about "I am not good enough" that is held in your subconscious program gets activated. You will notice that in your feelings, body sensations, thoughts, and energy as a resistance, an inner wall, a hesitation, or just plain disbelief.

But if you are introducing the *possibility*—"*What if* I am good enough?"—your feelings, body sensations, thoughts, and energy will show you what that experience would be like.

When you ask yourself, "What if I am good enough? How would I feel if I were good enough?" you might notice that you are more relaxed, sense more spaciousness, and feel more joyful and more open toward others.

When you ask, "What if . . . ?" and "How would I feel if . . . ?" it is important not to try to figure out the answer through thinking. Instead, choose to be the observer of your body sensations, your feelings, your thoughts, and your energies. Watch them shift and let *them* show you how you would feel.

Your body sensations, feelings, thoughts, and energies are the messengers of your subconscious. And it is in your subconscious that you want to change your limiting beliefs!

Questions that keep you stuck and questions that move you forward

You know when you do an online search for something and you don't get the information you are looking for? You quickly change your question and your keywords to try to get the information you need. The same is true for asking yourself questions when you feel stuck in your personal life and you want to figure things out and move forward. The key to getting the right information is asking the right questions and being clear about where you want to receive the information from.

There are several "data banks" that you can access when you ask yourself questions:

- Your personal data bank, which holds information about your old experiences, programs, patterns, and beliefs.
- The data bank of your higher wisdom, your soul.
- The data bank of the collective consciousness of humanity (more on that in Part III).
- The data bank of different consciousnesses in the unseen realm.
- The data bank of Higher Consciousness, God, Source, Creator, Universe (whichever name feels right and most comfortable to you).

The answers you get will be different for each data bank you are accessing. The words you use, your feeling state, and the energy you are asking your questions from will also influence the answers you get.

When you ask, "What is wrong with me that I can't do this job/can't make the time to meditate every day/can't stick to my diet?" you might get thoughts of what is wrong with you. You might sense a confirmation that there is something wrong with you. You asked your personal data bank of old patterns and beliefs. You got answers to your questions, but you didn't really get what you were looking for.

So you change your questions and keywords to get a better result.

You ask:

"What do I need to do to be able do this job?"

"What do I need to know to be able to do this job?"

"How do I need to feel to make time to meditate every day?"

Chapter 18 | The Power of "What if..."

"What do I need to believe to be able to stick to my diet?"

You are now asking forward-moving questions. You are asking the data banks of your higher wisdom and/or the collective consciousness of humanity and/or of the Highest Consciousness. You will get answers that support you in what you need and want.

Other negative questions that keep you stuck in limitation are ones like:

"Why can't I have ... ?"

"Why can't I be ... ?"

"Why am I so stupid, so self-conscious, so insecure, so ... ?"

When you ask these questions, "Why can't I have ... ?" and "Why can't I be ... ?" with thoughts of being stuck, with feelings of defeat and powerlessness, they'll keep you in the repetition of the past. The answers that you get will give you reasons and confirmations for being stuck. They won't give you answers for moving forward.

Exploration and questions about the past and past trauma have their place. When you come with the intention of really wanting to discover the source of your limiting patterns and beliefs, you come from curiosity and openness in your questions. The answers to these questions will let you remember past situations and experiences. They will help you to realize how you feel now is connected to how you felt in your family, at school, and with your friends. They will guide you to the sources of your limiting beliefs.

A powerful question about your past — asked with curiosity and the knowing that the answer will lead you forward — is "How did this belief come into my life?" The answer to this question opens up a deeper awareness and understanding of the sources of that belief. The answers will often show you that the belief is not actually personal but is shared collectively and/or passed down in the lineage of your family. The answers will move you into empowerment to heal trauma and shift limitations; they will open the door to compassion and empathy for yourself and the traumatic circumstances that created your limiting belief.

What other questions move you forward?

At times, when you are unclear about how to move forward with an inner or outer goal, you can simply ask, "What is the next step for me to take?" Consciously decide which data banks you want to address with your question. Then be receptive to receiving an answer. The answer might come in words, thoughts, or insights. It might come in the form of a book, a podcast, or a conversation with someone. If the answer comes to you in words or thoughts right away but sounds too big or vague, ask for more detail until you get an answer that shows you a step you can take right now.

Other questions that move you forward are questions that help you experience what you want to have, be, and do. These questions activate your feelings, images, thoughts, and body sensations, showing you what it would be like to have what you are asking for. They are similar to the imagining of your childhood. They are the "What if . . . " and other questions that open the possibility of a new reality for you.

"What if this belief, that I am not good enough, is actually not true?"

"How would I feel being good enough?"

"How would I feel right now imagining that I am good enough?"

"How would I feel knowing that I deserve to be happy?"

"What if I could have a job that truly fulfills me?"

"What if I could love myself?"

Chapter 18 | The Power of "What if..."

"What if I felt safe being who I truly am?"

"What if I am actually loved for who I am?"

When you ask questions like these, you open up potentiality and invite possibility. You also invite your innate state of being to come alive. You invite the knowing of your heart and soul to answer your questions. Your whole being goes on an inner "online" search to find the answers to your questions.

Let's take the question "What if this belief, that I am not good enough, is actually not true?" When you play with this potentiality and possibility, let go of trying to find the answer intellectually. You could add the question "How would I feel being good enough?" Sense your feelings, body sensations, energies, and images as the answer to your question. When you *feel* your feelings and body sensations, *sense* energies, and *see* images, then you *know* the answer. You could then, but just then, add a question that invites your thoughts to give an answer: "What would that mean for my relationship/work/life...?" And after that you can continue using the answer from your thinking mind for another feeling question. Let's say your thoughts tell you that "Being good enough would mean that I would be more loving in my relationships/more confident at work/more forward moving in my life..." You can then ask, "What would it *feel* like to be more loving in my relationships/more confident at work/more forward-moving in my life?" Then focus on *feeling* the answer to this question. Your brain will create neural connections that transmit the felt information of your senses. You are now creating new neural pathways. The felt information of your senses will change the neural network in your brain.

The more often you play with the potentiality and possibility of your question and answers and the longer you stay with these feelings, body sensations, energies, and images, the more neural connections transmitting this information are created, and over time it will be easier for you to access this information.

It is actually the same process that occurs when you build and practise any new skill. The ability of your brain and neurons to change in this way is called neuroplasticity.

Here are steps you can follow:

1. **Ask your question.** For example, "How would I feel right now if I were good enough?" (Replace this example with a question that is relevant to you.)

2. **Don't try to *think* of the answer. Instead, let your body sensations and your feelings *show you* the answer.** Also, become aware of images, intuitive thoughts, and energies. You might feel parts of your body relaxing. You might notice that you are taking deeper breaths. You might become aware of your heart softening, of a lighter energy in your chest, and you might feel more loved and more loving. You might notice the thought "I feel safe."

3. **Expand these feelings spatially.** Now allow these feelings of relaxation to expand from that place you first noticed them to more areas of your body. Allow the softening of your heart, for instance, to expand into the softening of your whole chest, your neck, your shoulders, your belly . . . It is more an allowing for that to happen than an active doing.

4. **Expand these feelings, timewise.** Stay with these sensations, feelings, energies, and images as long as you can. At some point your mind will come in and want to have its say. It might want to remind you of your to-do list for the day or why you shouldn't do this. It might bring in some old beliefs from your family or school that these things don't really work. When you notice your mind coming in like this, stop. Don't fight your mind. Thank it for its concerns. Acknowledge and celebrate for a moment the

beautiful inner experiences you just had and commit to getting back to it another time.

The more often you practise these steps, the more neurons transfer the information of your felt sense. They bundle up and build bigger neural pathways with the new information. This neural pathway you are creating holds your new reality of being good enough.

And the less you feel, think, and imagine the old information of "not being good enough," the faster the old path of neural connections transmitting *that* information will be disassembled. And your habit of going there will eventually weaken and diminish.

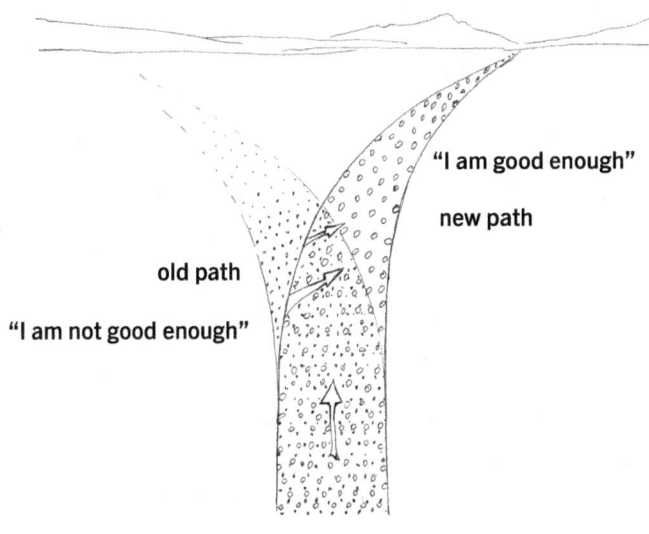

Creating a New Neural Pathway

Here on the West Coast of Canada, where I live, the underbrush of the woods is often salal bushes. The trails and paths through the woods that are most used are well established, visible, and easy to walk on. There are no salal bushes on these well-established paths. The trails that are less used are harder to follow. There are salal bushes everywhere, and you need to be very focused to make out the trail.

Creating a new path of neural connections is a little bit like creating a new path through the salal. It is different from walking habitually on an established path.

When you walk on an established path, your mind can wander, you can be unconscious about where you are walking. You can talk with your friend about things unrelated to where you are and still stay on the path.

When you create a new path, you have to be conscious, present, and aware, and you have to pay attention to the landmarks. Here is a big rock (body sensations) . . . and here is that moss-covered log (thoughts) . . . and here is that pond (feelings), etc.

When you want to get on that path next time, it will be similar but a little bit different. Don't try to have the same experience as last time. Don't try to feel, sense, and imagine the same as when you were there last time on your "What if . . . " experience path. Trying to create the same experience you had last time will not get you on the trail.

Instead, be present, aware, and conscious of the body sensations, feelings, and thoughts *this time*.

The pond might have more or less water (feelings), the moss on the log might now be a deep green or glitter with dewdrops (thoughts), and the big rock might have some bird droppings on it (body sensation) . . . or you might notice a little rock cairn made by someone else who has discovered this path and walked it as well.

Chapter 19

Getting Off the Cushion into Being Triggered

Have you ever experienced this?

You are in a beautiful meditation. You feel calm, peaceful, and loving. You experience expansiveness and a sense of Oneness with All-That-Is. You come out of the meditation, and your heart is open. You go about your day feeling good—until your partner, friend, coworker, boss, child, or parent says something to you. And you get triggered!

Gone is the sense of peace and calm, and you don't feel so loving anymore. You get really angry and reactive in your response to the other person. They're reactive as well. You both leave the room upset and fuming.

After you have calmed down a bit, you start feeling somewhat ashamed that you were so reactive. You are upset with yourself that you didn't stay in your expanded, loving, and spiritually open state—and you begin to doubt your spiritual growth.

Does this sound familiar? If so, you are not alone.

What happened?

During your meditation you let go of identifying with your body, your role, your work, your name. You let go of your human identification. And in that process, you also let go of your limiting beliefs!

When you went back to your everyday activity, you went back to your human identity, including your limiting beliefs. When the other person said something to you, the limbic part of your brain interpreted it as danger, and you got triggered. An old limiting belief got reactivated in you. That's all.

It does not mean anything about your spiritual growth—or that your meditation was not good, or that meditation does not work, or that you have to meditate more, or that you have to find a different spiritual path.

- Meditation alone does not change the subconscious programming from childhood.
- Meditation alone does not heal trauma and change limiting beliefs.
- Adding tools to your meditation practice can help you dissolve your limiting beliefs.

Our human limiting beliefs seem endless. One lifetime might not be long enough to clear them all one by one. But the more you clear your limiting beliefs the less you will buy into the illusion that you are something other than your divine, eternal, expanded Self living your life in a human body.

At some point you might want to choose to reprogram the deepest limiting belief in your subconscious programming—the belief that you are something other than your eternal divinity. This will go hand in hand with your meditation practice. It will support you in not identifying yourself as easily with your limiting beliefs when you get off the meditation cushion. It will support you in staying connected to your expanded consciousness when you go back to your everyday activities.

PART III

Shifting into Oneness

Out beyond ideas of wrongdoing and rightdoing there is a field.
I'll meet you there.

~ RUMI ~

(trans. Coleman Barks)

Dissolving limiting beliefs is not just about being able to live a life where we can make more money or have our dream job or a better relationship. It's not just about manifesting what we desire in the material world. On a deeper level it is about coming back to the truth of who we are. Dissolving our limiting learned and inherited beliefs about our deepest truth will help us shift back into Oneness. The beliefs that have kept us from living who we really are are personal and collective.

Limiting beliefs cause disconnection from ourselves, each other, and All-That-Is. This disconnection shows up in our personal lives and relationships. It shows up in our collective lives, where it is played out between social groups, gender groups, ethnic and racial groups, and nations.

Our experience of moving from separation into Oneness is determined by our beliefs—the supportive and the limiting beliefs we have about separation and Oneness. In order to move out of the personal and collective experiences of good and bad, lesser and higher, worthy and unworthy, we need to become aware of our beliefs about separation and Oneness. Then we can update them, just like we update our personal childhood beliefs.

We live in a time when to realize and live from Oneness with each other and All-That-Is is no longer for spiritual seekers alone. What if shifting out of disconnection is the next evolutionary step for humanity? What if we are called to shift into Oneness at this time in history? What if the survival of humanity depends on it?

Chapter 20

Three Realms and How They Are Interlinked

You can use the concept of realms to understand and navigate your experiences of separation and Oneness. Here we'll use the concept of the three following realms:

- The realm of infinite possibility—it is formless
- The realm of unseen forms
- The realm of seen forms

You are part of these three realms all the time. They are interconnected and in constant communication. You can learn to consciously choose your part in this communication. In order to do that you need to become aware of your beliefs.

Let's look at each of these three realms and explore your communication in them.

The realm of infinite possibility

There are countless names for this realm or reality. We can call it God, the Divine, Universe, Spirit, The Field, Highest Consciousness, Creator, Quantum Field, Source, Universal Energy, Highest Intelligence . . .

Which name do *you* use? Which name are you most comfortable with? If you like, use *your* preferred name for this reality as you read these pages. In various places I will use Field of Infinite Possibility, God, the Highest Consciousness, and the Divine.

The realm of infinite possibility is not bound in time and space. That means it is everywhere, all the time. There is no place, that we know of, where this realm is not present. We are part of this realm — all the time!

To perceive this reality of infinite possibility we have to move into an alpha or theta brainwave state. We *feel* this reality of Highest Consciousness through our inner perceptions and *sense* it through our conscious mind. We can *think* about this reality intellectually. To *know* that it is here can be helpful for the times we don't feel it. To deeply be in Oneness with the Highest Consciousness we have to *feel* and *sense* it.

The moment we name it and talk about what we feel and sense, we move out of the alpha/theta brainwave state into a beta brainwave state. In that moment our experience of Highest Consciousness moves from the realm of *infinite* possibility (what we sense) into *one* possible reality (what we describe with our words). That is what is meant by God being "unnamable." The moment you name it, it is not infinite anymore. It has shifted into *one* defined reality.

Let's imagine you had a beautiful experience in your meditation. You felt One with everything. You knew and felt yourself as consciousness. You were in an expanded state of awareness. Now you share your experience with your partner, friend, or meditation group, and in that moment you leave the alpha or theta brainwave state you were in during meditation and you move into a beta brainwave state. You leave the experience of the reality of infinite possibility and move into the reality of the defined form of your words.

You cannot be in your alpha and theta brainwave state (in which you experience Oneness) *and* in a beta brainwave state (in which you describe your experience) at the same time. So, when you put your experience of Highest Consciousness into words, you move from *direct knowing* into *knowledge about*.

Maybe when you were a child adults told you that God is in Heaven and we are on Earth. What we know now is that God is a field of consciousness that is everywhere. It is here in your body, in every one of your cells, in your energy field—and in everyone and everything else!

Maybe when you were a child the adults around you said, "God knows everything about you. God sees and hears everything." Often this was connected to the idea of a praising and punishing God, an old paradigm belief of a humanized God. What we know now is that this field of consciousness holds infinite possibilities. It mirrors your own vibrations. It reflects your thoughts, feelings, and beliefs as your own experiences. In that sense God sees, hears, and knows everything.

The realm of unseen forms

This realm holds the patterns and forms that cannot be perceived through your five senses, but rather with your sixth sense. It is the realm of consciousnesses that are invisible to our eyes. You might notice these consciousnesses of unseen forms and patterns as energies. Our thoughts, feelings, and beliefs are energetic forms and vibrations, and they live in this realm.

These patterns and forms of energy are not bound in time and space. You might have experienced that you can feel your own feelings you had in a different lifetime (not bound in time). You might sense that you picked up thoughts or feelings from another person in the apartment next to you, or maybe they picked up yours (not bound in space).

Your thoughts, feelings, and beliefs can be perceived by others, and you can perceive theirs—no matter where you are. We perceive these unseen forms unconsciously all the time. How well we perceive this energetic information and how aware we are of it depends on our inner "Wi-Fi" connection.

Not only do others perceive the energies of our thoughts, feelings, and beliefs in this realm of unseen forms, but also, and most importantly, the Field of Infinite Possibility perceives and reflects them and creates our experiences and reality.

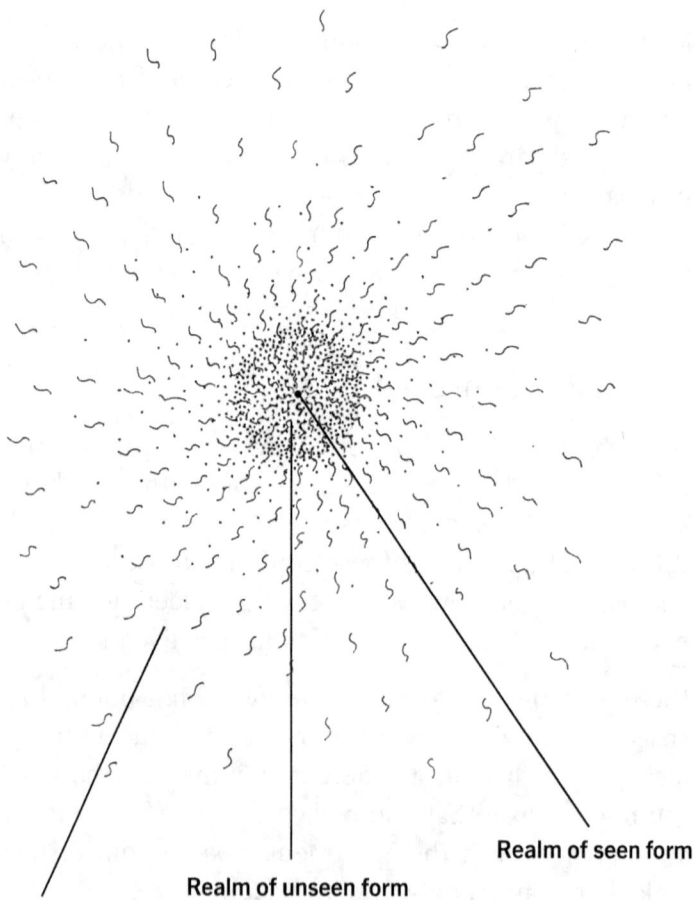

Realm of seen form
Realm of unseen form
Realm of infinite possibility

CHAPTER 20 | THREE REALMS AND HOW THEY ARE INTERLINKED

The realm of seen forms

This reality is the world of seen forms, of matter. In this world we perceive matter through our five senses. We see, hear, taste, smell, and feel forms that appear to us as matter.

And even though we live in a physical world of solid forms, quantum physicists have been informing us of the big illusion in this realm: *That there is no matter.* That what appears to us as matter is actually energy vibrating. It is hard to convince our eyes of this. They "stubbornly" see these forms as solid things — no energy moving here! If our knowledge and beliefs about this solidness changes, it might be possible that we'll be able to perceive the moving energy of "solid" forms.

The realm of seen form and matter is bound in time and space, at least with the belief system we operate in at this point in our evolution. The moment we are able to see, feel, and know matter as vibrating patterns of energy, we might be able to bilocate and maybe multilocate (well, that might be reaching a little too far into the future). For now, let's be more traditional and say this reality is bound in time and space . . . just for now.

So far in our Western culture we have been describing forms as animated or unanimated. We think of them as having life force or no life force. Since the Highest Consciousness is everywhere and in everything, wouldn't that mean all forms have life force in them?

We see human bodies, animal bodies, and plants as animated because we can see and perceive their movements and their life expressions. We describe rocks as inanimate because we perceive them as being still and unmoving "without life force." Because we can't perceive some of the more subtle expressions and movements of forms or the vibration of energy in matter, we draw the conclusion that there is no life force in some forms.

If we let go of making life force and consciousness in forms dependent on what we see, we might be more open to consciousness in "unmoving" matter. Even in human-made forms. "Things" are all created from elements of the Earth. What if we perceived our teapot, car, house, shirt, and dresser as having life force? And our technical devices? It might change how we relate to these forms of matter. We might change our relationship to these "things." We might take better care of them. We might be less assuming that resources are just there for us to take and use. We might have more gratitude. We might ultimately change our being here to a respectful and honouring relationship with the planet.

If you like, you could ask yourself some "What if . . . " questions: "What if I could I feel that there is consciousness in the table I am sitting at, in the water I am drinking, in the cup I am holding . . . ? What body sensations would I notice, what feelings would I feel?"

The process of communicating and co-creating within the three realms

Quantum physicists describe the energy of the realm of infinite possibility—the Quantum Field—as energy in wave formation. The moment this wave formation meets our perceptions, thoughts, feelings, and beliefs it collapses into a point. It collapses from infinite possibility into one probable reality. It shifts from unmanifested to manifested, from no-form to form. This form or pattern can appear as matter, and we experience it with our five senses. It also can appear as unseen forms, which we feel as feelings, think as thoughts, and perceive as energies with our sixth sense. In this process of co-creation, forms can also be "un-manifested," dissolved back into the formless, into the

CHAPTER 20 | THREE REALMS AND HOW THEY ARE INTERLINKED

energy of a wave formation. In this book we are focused on how we create and dissolve the forms and patterns of our beliefs.

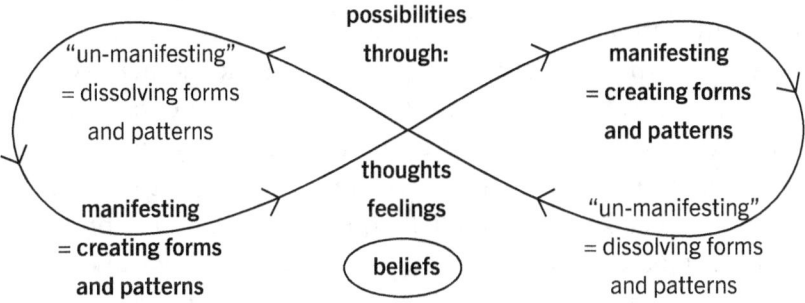

You communicate with this Field of Infinite Possibility all the time, whether you are conscious of it or not. You can notice this communication and be aware of what you communicate, or you can be unaware of it. You can choose your thoughts, feelings, and beliefs, or without much conscious choice you can keep them on their default setting of your subconscious programming.

In the vastness of creation, we humans have a tiny little part. In the co-creation of our own life, our experiences, our circumstances and environments we have a significant influence. We co-create consciously through communicating with the Field of Infinite Possibility by setting intentions, praying, visualizing, meditating, planning, and dreaming our visions and goals.

Unconsciously we co-create by communicating with the Field through our unconscious thoughts and feelings, which have their source in our subconscious beliefs. Some of these beliefs limit and hinder the creation and expression of what we want in our life. And some of these beliefs support the life we want to live.

The Field of Infinite Possibility, Highest Consciousness, is non-judgmental. It mirrors all vibrations. It all gets created, the "positive," the "negative," and the "indifferent."

Since what and how you communicate to the realm of infinite possibility is driven by your supportive and limiting beliefs, you need to be aware of your beliefs to have any real choice in this communication. You might *consciously* communicate a specific message to the Highest Consciousness, but the moment you let go of being aware of that message, your communication will continue *unconsciously*. Your thoughts and feelings might shift quickly, influenced by what you are experiencing in the moment and by your subconscious beliefs. These beliefs can support what you consciously communicated to the Field or they can contradict what you communicated. **To be congruent in your communication, you need to have your conscious communication backed by your beliefs. What you consciously communicate to the Field needs to be the same as what you subconsciously believe in order to co-create what you want to do, have, and be.**

Let's look at an example.

If you communicate consciously to the Field that you want a higher income, you might be very clear about how much more money you want. You might be using intentions, visualizations, vision boards, affirmations; you might have even written down your goals and dreams. But if you have the belief that you are not good enough to have that kind of money or that you don't deserve what you want, the underlying belief will be the strongest message you send to the Field of Infinite Possibility.

Incongruence between what you consciously communicate and what your beliefs communicate to the Field will co-create incongruent results. For example, as a result of your incongruent communication, you might get paid a bonus for a specific job but you don't get the salary raise you wanted.

Most of creation happens without us. Our place is to be in awe of the consciousness and power that creates the vastness of All-That-Is. Through miraculous processes it creates interconnectedness and balance of minuscule details, all of which we are only beginning to understand.

Chapter 21

The Collective Invisible Website

Just as we each have a personal invisible website, we also have a collective invisible website that we share with the whole of humanity. This invisible collective website also has a menu, posts, and blogs—pages with the collective beliefs we carry as humanity, posts with the current thoughts, feelings, and actions of all people on the planet, and blogs with our collective stories.

You could look at it as something like this:

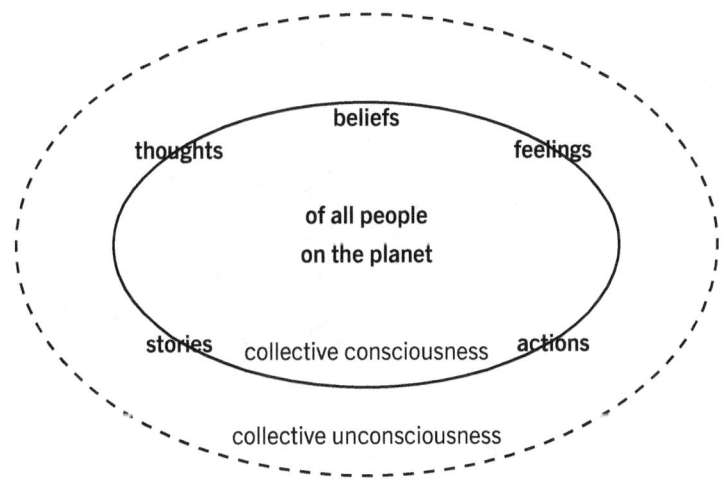

It's like a huge field of information. Everyone is linked to it—without any technical devices. Every one of our thoughts, our feelings, our beliefs, our actions, and the energy we invest in each of them contribute to the information in this collective field.

We are conscious of some of the information in the collective field, but we're unconscious of most of it. We can also call this huge invisible field of information the collective consciousness and collective unconsciousness of humanity.

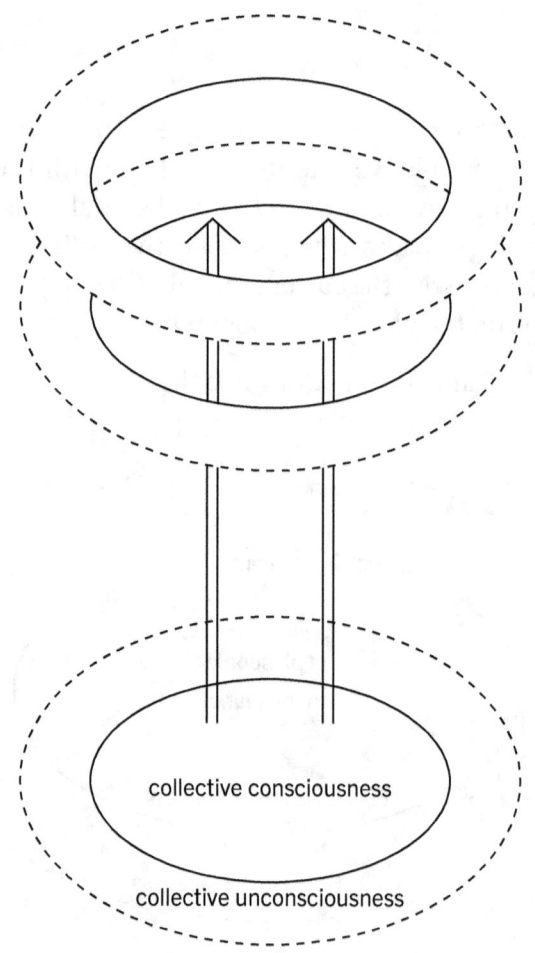

Collective Consciousness and Unconsciousness Shifting Over Time

CHAPTER 21 | THE COLLECTIVE INVISIBLE WEBSITE

This invisible collective consciousness and unconsciousness is constantly shifting in an evolutionary movement.

Over time, the information in it changes. What our great-grandparents and grandparents believed, we don't necessarily believe today. Our children and grandchildren are born into a different time—into a different field of collective information. They don't believe certain things anymore. Some menu items, posts, and blogs that the older generation might still be struggling with seem foreign or outdated to the younger generation. Other menu items, posts, and blogs are still affecting people of all ages.

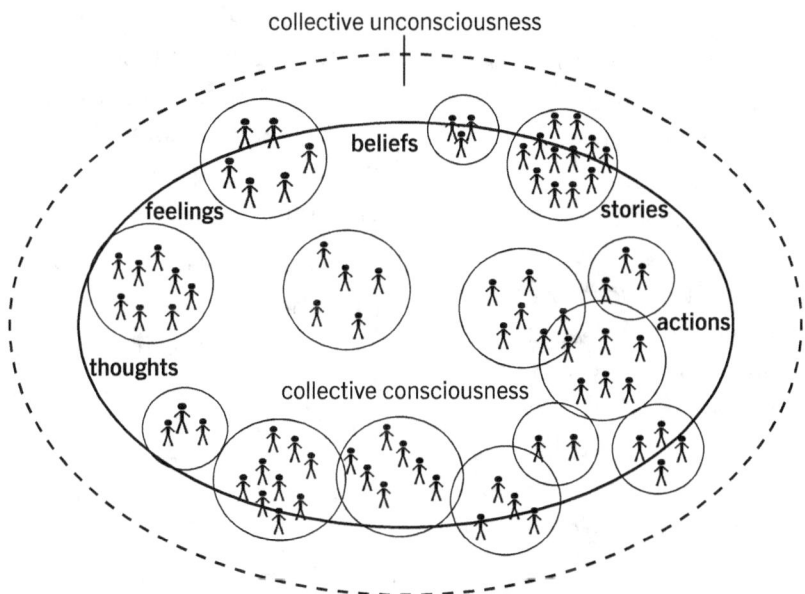

This collective website has pages holding information from many sub-websites of different groups. Group websites or group consciousnesses are created by different nations, different ethnic groups and races, different genders, different religions, groups of people with similar interests, and families and couples. Each one of us belongs to several of these groups and contributes information to their websites.

You might wonder why this collective field of information is important.

The information on our invisible websites affects the experiences in our lives. This is just as true for your personal life as it is for our collective experiences as humanity.

Our brain is—besides all its other functions—also a receiver station for information from the outside. Usually when we think of information from the outside we think of information we perceive with our five senses, which gets sent to and processed in our brain. But what if our brain also responds to information it can receive *without* using our five senses, data that is held in some field of information, some field of consciousness?

That would explain how people remember past-life experiences. It would explain how you can remember people, places, and events from a time when you had a different physical brain than you have today! It also might explain how you can have beliefs in this life that you actually formed in another lifetime. It would explain how you are linked to the data of the invisible fields of information.

> *You might sometimes feel powerless and without influence over the collective events of our time. But however small your influence feels, you are **never** without it.*
> *With your thoughts, your feelings, your actions, and your beliefs you **always** influence the collective invisible website of humanity, out of which our human stories, experiences, and events are co-created.*

You might sometimes feel powerless and without influence over the collective events of our time. But however small your influence feels, you are *never* without it.

Chapter 21 | The Collective Invisible Website

With your thoughts, your feelings, your actions, and your beliefs, you *always* influence the collective invisible website of humanity, out of which our human stories, experiences, and events are co-created.

The moment you dissolve a limiting belief it is "posted" not only on your personal invisible website but also on the collective website. And with this post you support and help others to dissolve their limiting beliefs!

When you go through the process of dissolving a limiting belief, you are also taking the trauma energy out of the experiences that created the limiting belief. The past traumas, personal and collective, exist as information in the collective field. And whether a limiting belief originated from a trauma you or someone else experienced, the moment you dissolve it, you reduce the trauma energy in the fields of information. You change the information on both your personal *and* the collective invisible website. This will create a shift in your personal life, and it will also contribute to the shift of consciousness in humanity.

Each one of us not only *influences* the collective field of information, we are also *being influenced by* it. Most of the time this happens unconsciously. When you become conscious of what you are influenced by, you can choose what you want to do with that information.

One morning some years back I woke up feeling somewhat grumpy and low. There was nothing I was aware of that could have caused me to feel like that. I had gone to bed feeling happy and content. I became curious about a possible source of my mood. It was a grey, rainy morning. I thought of the collective thoughts and feelings that end up being posts on collective sub-websites. I live on an island with around ten thousand people. That made it easy for me to think of the collective feelings and thoughts of all the islanders. I thought of the fact that people get depressed and feel low when it rains and the sky is grey.

I started an experiment. I said out loud, "I am disengaging from all thoughts and feelings of all people on the island right now." Guess what happened? In an instant my mood lifted. My grumpiness and feeling low were gone! I had been unconsciously influenced by the posts (feelings and thoughts about the weather) on the collective group website of the islanders.

You might be familiar with feeling a certain way without being able to find the source and reason for it in your personal life. It is quite possible that in those moments you have picked up posts from smaller or larger group websites while you were riding a bus, stuck in stop-and-go traffic, or driving on the highway. Malls, churches, schools, offices, businesses all have their own fields of energetic information. They all influence you. Bigger occurrences that happen in our communities, towns, cities, countries, and globally on the planet create thoughts and feelings in each person that end up as information on the invisible collective website. This is true for "good feeling" events as well as emotionally challenging events.

If you feel a certain way that you don't like and you can't find any cause for this feeling in your personal life, chances are that you have been influenced by some information in the collective field.

We know from quantum physics that energy follows thoughts and energy follows your words. You can use this law to disengage from the information you picked up.

- You can simply say, "I disengage from the energetic information of the highway/the subway/the bus/the mall/the store/the school/the office . . . " or whatever the source is. Or you could say, "I ask that all the energies (thoughts, feelings, and beliefs) that I picked up today leave my body and my energy field right now." And if you like, you can add, "And I ask that these energies (thoughts, feelings, and beliefs) go into the highest healing."

Then just see how you feel afterward.

If nothing has changed:

- The energies (thoughts, feelings) might have been yours after all.
- You might have a belief that you can't let these energies go. For some reason you are not allowing yourself to let them go, and for some reason you have to hold onto them. Be curious about these limiting beliefs and start the process of dissolving them.

If you feel lighter, more spacious, happier, clearer, and more yourself:

- You have let go of the information that influenced you!

Take a moment to allow yourself to realize and *feel* that you are constantly influenced by information on the collective invisible websites of humanity—and that *you* constantly influence that information as well!

You know how you can observe patterns in nature that are the same on a microscopic level as they are on the macroscopic level? The same patterns show up as tiny little forms, smaller than you can see with your eyes, and as huge landscapes and vast cosmic forms and patterns.

The same is true for human patterns. You might sense a fleeting little thought or a feeling that has an energy of fear, abuse, contempt, or put-down. That thought or feeling might not have anything much to do with what you are actively living in your life. It might be something you are sensing through your connection to the whole of humanity's collective consciousness and unconsciousness. And the patterns that you notice as tiny little feelings or energies you can also see as patterns played out in huge collective traumas. The moment you have awareness of these patterns you can contribute to changing them. You can shift these fleeting little thoughts or feelings you are sensing, and in doing so, you contribute to shifting how these patterns manifest on the larger scale.

The same is true, of course, for little thoughts and feelings you are noticing that have the energy of love, connection, collaboration, caring, and honouring. They too are something you might sense through your connection to the collective field of information. And in the same way, the moment you are aware of that, you have a choice. You can choose to expand and strengthen these patterns of thoughts and feelings that inform the collective field. In this way you have influence over what plays out for the whole of humanity.

You can ask yourself:

"What do I tend to pick up?"

"What am I putting into the field?"

The more conscious you are about this, the more choices you have. When you are aware, you can consciously choose the information you want to put into the collective field of consciousness. And you can choose more consciously what you want to do with the information that you pick up. With your conscious choices, you contribute to making the collective unconsciousness smaller and the collective consciousness larger. In this way you have a voice and an influence over what happens on this planet.

We are all players in this collective field! We are all connected in the patterns we create! When we realize that our personal patterns are the same as the collective, we know we have influence not only to shift our personal lives but also to shift our collective experience as humanity.

Chapter 22

Our Experiences in the Three Realms and Separation Trauma

Earlier we talked about the three realms. Let's have a closer look at the experiences you might have in each one of them.

Depending on which realm you identify with, you experience a different "you," a different "self."

When you identify with the realm of seen forms (the realm of matter), you experience yourself as your physical body, separate from others. You might identify with the things you own and have in your life.

When you identify with the realm of unseen form, you experience yourself as your thoughts and feelings, your body sensations, and your beliefs. And it feels like they are "you."

When you identify with these two realms, you experience your limitations. You label what you have, your body and your worldly goods, and what you think, feel, sense, and believe as "good" or "bad." In this identification you focus on meeting your needs. And you often judge the experience of your needs being fulfilled as "good" and the experience of your needs not being fulfilled as "bad." And most of all, you draw conclusions about your worthiness, lovability, good-enoughness . . . out of these "good" or "bad" experiences. Your life becomes a yo-yo experience of ups and downs. You experience duality.

The realm of matter/seen forms and realm of unseen forms are the realms of impermanence. That means nothing lasts, everything is temporary, everything is in the process of change. The forms that are created, whether they are visible or invisible, change constantly. There's nothing to hold onto as permanent. Often the longing and search for wholeness and for the real "you" is a recurring experience in these realms.

When you identify with the realm of infinite possibility, you know yourself as consciousness, as expanded self, as unconditional love—One with All-That-Is!

This realm of Highest Consciousness is the realm of permanence. It is the unchanging reality of no forms, while holding and including all forms. Highest Consciousness holds infinite potentiality and possibility.

From this realm all your experiences in the realms of seen and unseen forms are created. This realm is your source of everything. When you identify with this realm you feel at home, you experience wholeness, Oneness, unconditional love, peace, calm, and joy. There is a sense that all your needs are met. You don't sense or feel any unmet needs. In fact, the whole concept of needs seems irrelevant and unimportant in this realm. You are present in the moment. All the limiting beliefs fall away. They just don't exist in this realm.

So why wouldn't you just stay in the experience of this realm?

Let's have a closer look at this by exploring the trauma of separation from this realm.

Every time we get separated from someone or something without choosing or agreeing to the separation, we experience trauma. Thinking back on your own life, you might remember people, places, and situations when you experienced this.

One trauma of separation that almost all human beings share is the experience of separation from the Divine, the Highest

Chapter 22 | Our Experiences in the Three Realms

Consciousness. We move into that apparent separation by being conditioned and programmed to believe "beliefs of separation." These beliefs basically say, "We are not divine, not sacred." They say that we are separate from the Highest Consciousness, and that our connection to the Divine is conditional. These beliefs are not really the truth. They have been made up by people throughout human history. But the moment we believe them, we feel separate from the Divine, the Highest Consciousness, and separate from who we truly are.

A lot has changed in the last several decades. Many people no longer believe the beliefs of separation as strongly as they once did. Personally and collectively we might not *think* that the beliefs "We are separate from the Highest Consciousness" and "We are separate from each other" are true anymore. More and more people are connected to the knowledge that we are all One. This knowledge, though, is mainly held intellectually and in the knowing of our hearts and souls, but *not* in our subconscious programming yet. In our subconscious programming the old limiting beliefs of separation are still dominant for most of us. These beliefs keep us in experiences of feeling separate from our Source, from our true being, from each other, and from All-That-Is.

Let's look at how we got here.

For most of us, this programming of the limiting beliefs of separation started right at birth. In Spanish, the term for giving birth, *dar a luz*, literally means "to give to light." Most of us were born into the dark, into the unawareness of the people receiving us. We were born into the inheritance of the darker, unconscious times of human history.

Most of us were not seen, recognized, or greeted as the divine beings we are when we came into this world. Instead we were seen as cute but incomplete human babies who needed to be formed and filled with information. And in this process of "being formed" and "being filled" we took on the thoughts, feelings, behaviours, and beliefs of our parents and other people present at the time of our upbringing.

Perhaps you've heard the story of the 4-year-old girl who—as witnessed by her parents—said to her baby brother, "Please tell me about God. I am starting to forget." This little girl was starting to do what most of us do. Surrounded by people who did not live their divinity, she was starting to forget her Oneness with The Divine.

What were the messages of separation that *you* might have learned to believe when you were growing up? Let's look at possible sources and scenarios of the messages:

- There were spoken and unspoken messages from the people around you whom you were dependent on for your survival and well-being. These messages said and implied that you are your body, your feelings, your thoughts, and your actions, and that in this defined form of your body you are something different than the Divine.

- There were messages from the Church and/or religion that said you were born sinful, you were not good enough to be with God. You had to improve, be better, and be forgiven your "badness" in order to be worthy of and received by God.

- Perhaps you remember experiences when, as a child, you felt, thought, and behaved from your true soul being. It might have been that you were innocently excited and curious about something. Or you were in awe, amazed, and fascinated by the miracles of a little bug, worm, or spider. You were one with All-That-Is. However, the people around you did not meet you in your innocence, excitement, curiosity, and awe, but—if it went well— they mildly smiled at you. And if it did not go well, they ridiculed you, and you got the impression you were doing something wrong or bad.

- Perhaps as a child you felt, sensed, saw, or knew some information about people, animals, plants, or energies of places and were humiliated for it, laughed at, or told you were making things up.

- So, you learned that it is not safe to live your "soul you" and that there is something wrong with you if you do. You formed beliefs about that, and more and more, you let go of living in the state of your true being.

- There might be memories, fears, and beliefs from previous lifetimes. Memories from lifetimes when you were killed for wanting to live your Divine-connected state. These memories and fears can show up in your subconscious programming as beliefs like "I am not safe living in my light and highest state of being."

- You might also hold beliefs that others and outside situations can take you out of your state of Oneness. You learned these beliefs growing up, when you experienced many, many times that the words, energies, and behaviours of others pulled you out of your true-being state.

- You might also have beliefs that you *need* certain other people and settings to shift you *into* your state of Oneness (like a teacher, a guru, your soulmate, or your spiritual group . . .). It is true that it can be easier to experience your true being when you are around certain people, in certain situations, atmospheres, or energies. But it is your own beliefs that cause you to think you need that in order to shift into your state of Oneness. Ultimately it is your own beliefs that allow others to pull you out of or shift you into your state of Oneness.

- When others inflicted little or big physical, emotional, sexual, or energetic injuries on you, it wounded the sacredness of who you are. You interpreted this as, "This must mean I am not sacred," "It must mean I am not who I know I am," or "It must mean I am not safe to be who I really am," and a limiting belief was formed about yourself and others.

- Maybe you inherited a limiting belief from someone generations before you whose sense of sacredness was wounded.

- And there are all the limiting beliefs we talked about in previous chapters—core beliefs about not being loved, not-being-good-enough, not being wanted, being excluded, being less than, being unworthy—in all variations of these beliefs. All of these limiting beliefs ultimately create a sense of separation.

When we were not seen and treated as divine and when we learned messages of separation, we unconsciously translated it to mean:

"I cannot be who I am."

"I am not safe being who I am."

"I am not divine."

"I am not sacred."

"I am not truly loved."

"I am separate from others."

"I am not one with all."

In its essence, every relational traumatic experience is being seen as, spoken to, and treated as "not sacred," "not divine." It can be as small as not being noticed, being ignored, or not being validated, or it can be larger traumatic experiences of impactful emotional, physical, and sexual abuse.

Chapter 22 | Our Experiences in the Three Realms

For me, the biggest trauma we suffer in our lives is the trauma of separation. The trauma of experiencing and believing that we are separate from each other and everything around us. Of being separate from our soul, our Source, our divine consciousness.

> *Anxiety, fear, despair, depression, hate, anger, and terror are gone the moment we step into the experience of the realm of infinite possibility, Highest Consciousness.*

I think this is the biggest trauma that we as human beings have experienced individually and collectively for thousands of years, and we experience it over and over again in small and big ways. The pain and suffering of feeling separate from the Divine and feeling disconnected from ourselves, each other, and everything around us is tremendous. **I believe this disconnection is the source of all anxiety, fear, despair, depression, hate, anger, rage, and terror.**

What we create on this planet is still influenced by our limiting beliefs. These beliefs show up in our thoughts, feelings, unmet needs, and behaviours and actions. When we have limiting beliefs about ourselves, we also have them about others. For instance, when we believe we are unworthy or more worthy than another, we play that out with others in our personal lives. We play that out collectively when we see our social group, our gender group, our racial and ethnic group, or our nation as unworthy or more worthy than another.

Imagine a time when we shift out of this!

Anxiety, fear, despair, depression, hate, anger, and terror are gone the moment we step into the experience of the realm of infinite possibility, Highest Consciousness. There, every person, every being, all forms are part of the Highest Consciousness. The disconnect from ourselves, others, and All-That-Is is gone the moment we step out of separation and into Oneness.

PART III | SHIFTING INTO ONENESS

The moment you step out of separation and into Oneness it is easy to treat yourself with kindness, love, understanding, and actions that are caring—and it is easy to do the same for others.

Chapter 23

Shifting Out of Separation into Oneness

You might have been on your path to Oneness, to living your true beingness for a while. You might call it being your authentic self. You might call it listening to your Higher Self. You might call it being guided by Source or the Universe. You might call it being in your Higher Consciousness. Or these thoughts and ideas might be fairly new to you.

You might have developed your ways of entering the state of Oneness, feeling your soul, and being guided by your heart.

And still you are searching and not quite there yet . . .

Right now, at this time on our planet, most of us are living some experience of separation as a manifestation of learned limiting beliefs. Even though we personally and collectively have found many ways of entering the state of Oneness, feeling our true selves, and experiencing states of Higher Consciousness, we don't live our daily lives from there yet.

The teachings of Eastern spiritual traditions have had a tremendous influence on Western culture in the last decades in terms of finding ways to enter the state of consciousness. Meditation and yoga have become mainstream now. To meditate and do yoga individually and in groups is a big step in the collective journey into the consciousness of Oneness.

But as we know now, if what we are doing is not backed by our beliefs, we will fall back to our default setting! That means that when you use ways of getting into the state of consciousness and Oneness, but you still have your learned and inherited beliefs of separation, your subconscious programming will pull you back out of that state into *its truth*—into separation. In order for your ways of entering the state of Oneness to create a lasting shift, they must be backed by supportive beliefs.

Remember, when what you *want consciously* and what you *believe unconsciously* are incongruent, you will get incongruent results. This is what you most likely have been experiencing on your spiritual path. You most likely have been experiencing constant shifting from being in Higher Consciousness states back to your limited self in your everyday life.

So, we have:

- **doors and entranceways**—the strategies, ways, and methods that get us into Oneness, into Highest Consciousness—and
- **beliefs** that either back up or sabotage us being in Oneness.

Let's look at this more closely.

Doors and entranceways into Oneness and into the realm of Highest Consciousness

There are many doors and entranceways for this shift into Oneness and Highest Consciousness. Each one of us needs to find our own door, our own path. Each personal door, entranceway, and path is unique. And within their uniqueness they also share certain elements.

Feelings and ways of being

When we are in Oneness, we experience **certain feelings and ways of being**.

Chapter 23 | Shifting Out of Separation into Oneness

Here are some that are often experienced:

peace

calm

compassion

acceptance

nonjudgment

unconditional love

gratitude

joy

harmony

understanding

ease

Each feeling state and way of being can be a door and entranceway to the state of Oneness. They themselves are not the state of Oneness. Each one is an aspect of the whole, beautiful in itself but just one experience, one expression of the Highest Consciousness state. These feeling states themselves are not *it*.

If you use one of these feeling states as an entranceway to Oneness, be conscious of the energy you do it with. If you focus on these feeling states in order to improve or fix yourself, to be better, or "to get there," you ultimately will stay in the experience of separation. Sometimes you might notice that you are trying to do the "right spiritual" thing. You are focusing on being loving, kind, and good, but it feels a bit forced or strained. When you notice that happening, become curious about separation beliefs that you might still have in your subconscious programming. You might be trying to prove these beliefs wrong. They might show up as beliefs of good and bad, worthy and unworthy, better and lesser. When you are in the state of

Oneness, you don't need to focus on being good, kind, loving, connected—you just *are*. When you bring your attention and focus to *feeling* these states without attachment to an outcome, each one can be a beautiful door and entranceway to Oneness.

The moment you are living the experience of Oneness, you don't need to focus on any of these feelings and states of being—you just *are* them!

Falling in love

A door and entranceway to the state of Oneness you most likely are familiar with is **falling in love**. In this state you let go of judgment and see the other in their true being-ness. You are in a state of unconditional love. You see from your heart instead of from the learned beliefs of your programmed mind.

You, too, are seen in your true beingness by the other. There is no judgment of good and bad, right and wrong. There is only love.

. . . Until you let go of the love state and buy into the limiting beliefs again.

That usually happens when you start defining the relationship with the person you fell in love with. The moment you give them the role of your boyfriend, girlfriend, partner, wife, husband, you start applying to them your learned beliefs about how to relate to the people closest to you to. The beliefs you learned growing up. You buy into your and the other's limiting *and* supportive beliefs about being a boyfriend/girlfriend, a partner, and a husband/wife. You start reading the information on your and their invisible websites, and you start playing out that information with each other.

. . . And with that, you leave the unconditional love state of Oneness.

CHAPTER 23 | SHIFTING OUT OF SEPARATION INTO ONENESS

Meditation, yoga, conscious breathing, music and sounds, dance, nature, creating art

Other doors and entranceways to the state of Oneness can be **meditation, yoga, conscious breathing, music and sounds, dance, nature, and creating art.** These are activities that can take you out of the beta brainwave state and move you into alpha and theta.

It is not the modality or activity itself that takes you into a state of Oneness. I am sure you have experienced times when you were meditating, doing yoga or conscious breathing, out in nature, or engaged in artistic activities, and found it pleasant, fun, and energizing—but with no state of Oneness in sight.

So, what is it about these modalities and activities that *can* shift you into Oneness?

It's the shift from beta brainwave activity to alpha and theta brainwave frequencies. You move into alpha and theta frequencies when you focus on body sensations, when you are present in the moment, when you let go of thinking about past and future, and when you don't buy into the thoughts of your mind. You could summarize it as "letting go of your mind and coming to your senses."

- **Meditation and yoga** move your focus inward and into an awareness of body sensations, into deep inner-feeling states in the present moment.
- **Conscious breathing** brings you into deep connection with your inner body sensations and into the present moment.
- **Nature** does not hold limiting thought patterns of the past, present, or future. It just is. It is in a state of Oneness—and invites you into it.
- **Music, sounds, and dance** all connect you to the present moment and to body awareness.

- **Artistic activities** often bring your focus into the present moment. You let go of the identification with past and future.

"What if nothing has a name?"

One day many years ago, I was driving on one of our island roads and asked myself, "What if nothing has a name?" Within a second I felt connected to everything around me in a field of Oneness I was part of. I could not think of a name for anything I saw. I felt like a newborn, one with all.

This powerful "What if . . . " question moves you directly into your right-brain perception and an alpha brainwave state.

If you like, try it out right now. What do *you* notice? What is *your* experience when you ask that question: "What if nothing has a name?"

You might know your personal doors and entranceways into being in Highest Consciousness. Or you might just discover them or learn new ones. And you might have experienced many times shifting into Oneness and dropping out of it again. You might have felt sad, disappointed, or frustrated when that happened.

What pulled you out of Oneness? Most likely limiting beliefs. Beliefs of being separate and beliefs of not being able to live your daily life from the state of Oneness.

Beliefs of being separate

When we received messages of separation, we started to believe we *are* separate.

We looked at these messages in chapter 22, Our Experiences in the Three Realms and Separation Trauma, where we discussed separation trauma.

Chapter 23 | Shifting Out of Separation into Oneness

Let's add some other aspects to them here:

- Sometimes when we were growing up we learned through cultural beliefs, religious beliefs, or both that someone other than ourselves has the authority in the knowing of and connection to God. That we need someone else (a priest, minister, guru, enlightened person) to be our link to the Highest Consciousness, to the Divine. We have collectively played out this story for many, many hundreds of years through the domination of Christian religions and Churches in our daily lives.

- Limiting beliefs of that story sound and look like: "The priest/guru/enlightened person has the authority over the knowing and knowledge of God. I don't." These beliefs sound a little bit like childhood beliefs and experiences: "My parents said . . . , they know what is right."

- You might have had experiences where you followed a certain spiritual teaching, a guru, an enlightened person, or a spiritual group and gave your power over to them. You let go of having your own authority over the knowledge of your Higher Self and your connection to the Highest Consciousness.

But if the Highest Consciousness, the Divine, God is inside you—inside each person, each being—and is everywhere, the authority and communication with that consciousness cannot be outside of you. And with each being on this planet being unique, they will also have their unique communication with that Highest Consciousness.

We are coming out of hundreds of years of being influenced by Christian religions that had the premise "You have to be good in order to be worthy of God." Some of our childhood beliefs sound similar: "If I am good enough, my parents will want me/love me/see me/keep me safe . . . "

The idea of having to be good, of having to improve, of needing to be better in order to be in Oneness will always keep you in separation. This belief of needing to be fixed, to be healed, to improve yourself will always repeat the story of being in the Garden of Eden and falling out of it—the story that tells you that if you are good, you are "in," and if you are bad, you are "out." If you improve something, you are only "in" until you find the next "flaw" in you that needs to be healed. What a human-made concept.

It is true that in certain feeling states—those feeling states that in the past we might have labelled "bad"—you cannot *feel* God, you cannot *feel* the Highest Consciousness. But that does not mean you are not worthy of the Divine or that you are separate from the Divine. You are *always* an expression of Highest Consciousness. You are *always* divine and one with everything, whether you feel it or not.

When you read this, you might think, "I don't have these beliefs. I know that I am one with everything. I know that God/Source is inside me. I know that the Divine is here for me all the time. I know that I don't have to improve to be part of the Divine."

Yes, you do know that. You do know it in your intellectual knowledge, and you do know it in your heart-and-soul-knowing, and there might be part of your conditioned and programmed subconscious that does not know it yet.

- It could be that there is an absorbed belief within you that you have to improve and be good in order to deserve being in Oneness—even though your intellect knows that is not true.
- It could be that there are beliefs from childhood that you are your body, your thoughts, your feelings, your achievements—even though your soul and heart know that is not true.

- It could be that you have an old passed-down limiting belief from the Church, for example, that told you your body is bad and sinful—even though your heart knows that is not true.

So, be curious about the messages of your subconscious. Remember, the way your subconscious communicates with you is through your feelings, your body sensations, your thoughts, and your experiences. Listen to their messages.

You can apply the information from chapter 6, How Do You Find Your Beliefs, to help you find your subconscious separation beliefs.

Beliefs about not being able to live your daily life from the state of Oneness

You might be shifting more and more effortlessly into the state of Oneness. But somehow it's hard to live your daily life from there.

You might have had experiences where you felt deep inner shifts in a workshop. Or you were in a meditation retreat where your heart opened wide, you felt connected to All-That-Is, and you lived unconditional love. And when you came back into your everyday life you didn't know how to live from these inner states of expansion and connectedness. For a little while you held onto them, but over time you went back to your "normal" state of being.

You might become aware that these experiences are connected to thoughts and beliefs like:

"I can't live in Oneness when others around me believe in duality."

"The energy of others and the world is so overpowering, it pulls me out of my Oneness state."

"I don't know how to live in Oneness and be in my body all the time."

"This goal is too big."

"I can't/I'm not allowed/I don't deserve to be connected to the Highest Consciousness and Oneness all the time in my daily life."

"It's not safe to live in unconditional love in this world."

"If I let go and lived from Oneness, everything would fall apart."

"If I lived from Oneness, I would lose the sense of who I am in my daily life."

"If I lived from Oneness, I would lose control. It would not feel safe."

"I am afraid of the unknown."

"I don't know how to live my daily life from Oneness."

Where do these beliefs come from?

They come from your childhood experiences and your parents' and your ancestors' experiences, which were influenced by cultures and religions.

Let's look at how Christian religions and teachings in particular have contributed to the sense of separation between our daily life and divinity.

In Christian religions there is a story that God is in Heaven and we as humans are on Earth. That God is up there and we are down here. That we have to strive to be up there and that at some point God will reach down to us. That God will have mercy on us.

When I was growing up there was a German children's prayer *"Lieber Gott mach mich fromm, dass ich in den Himmel komm,"*

CHAPTER 23 | SHIFTING OUT OF SEPARATION INTO ONENESS

which translates to "Dear God, make me pious, so that I can come to Heaven."

Because of this old story and old false subconscious beliefs, which we are still holding, we collectively and personally have patterns of looking *outside* of ourselves for Oneness, for happiness, for connection, for the Divine. These old false subconscious beliefs make it hard for us to be present here, now, in our daily life, living in our divinity and Oneness.

Instead we look for our true home outside of ourselves. We look for it in other people, in methods of healing, in searching for spiritual paths. We look for it in finding our purpose. We look for it in the future. We believe that there is a time in the future when we will finally be good enough/fixed or healed enough/advanced enough on our spiritual path to be in "Heaven" and so we busy ourselves trying to figure out how we can get there.

If the Divine would be somewhere "out there" according to those old beliefs, it would mean that when we are in connection with ourselves, we are not with the Divine. And you might have experienced that actually the opposite is true. That when you are really connected and present with yourself, feeling your body, you are sensing the Divinity in you and your connection with All-That-Is! As the influence of Eastern spiritual traditions has grown stronger in the West, people from Western cultures have started to look more and more inside for Oneness, for God, for connection with All-That-Is. And we know now that it is through our body awareness that we can enter the state of Oneness. It is not a shift in an up-and-down location (Heaven and Earth) but a shift in frequency that lets us *feel* our divinity, and that frequency shift happens *inside* us.

In Christianity-influenced societies we are coming out of many hundreds of years where the Divine, the connection to God, the sacred was "reserved" for the Church, saints, monks, nuns, and monasteries. The earthly everyday life was considered lower, sinful, and separate from God and the Divine. The body, the flesh, was often labelled as bad and sinful.

We don't believe intellectually in that division of sacred and worldly life anymore. "Non-sacred" actions of Churches, monks, and nuns are more widely known. And yet there are still sub- and unconscious beliefs of separation of the sacred and earthly life that can make it difficult for us to live our daily life from the Highest Consciousness state.

One of the ways that these beliefs about separation of the sacred and earthly life shows up is in our disconnect from our bodies. Those old beliefs about our body being bad, too dense, and sinful still influence our daily experiences in and with our bodies.

It can seem almost easier to *know* that we are eternal consciousness than to *see, feel, and treat* our bodies as sacred.

If you want, take a moment to feel what your relationship to your body is like. Do you fully sense your body as being sacred, as being divine? Or is there a little hesitation, some sadness, an energetic wall you can sense? A small notion of not liking something about your body, of needing to improve it, making it better somehow? Or thoughts that you need to leave your body to feel your sacredness?

We live in a time of our human evolution when we are called to live embodied enlightenment, and that means staying present in our body when we are in our conscious connection to All-That-Is. We live in a time when we are called to live in Oneness—and that includes living in Oneness with our bodies!

But if we hold subconscious beliefs about our body being bad, sinful, too dense, not good enough, and separate from God, it is hard to stay in the connection to our divine being that is present in our body. It is hard to live our daily lives connected to All-That-Is. Then our subconscious separation beliefs pull us out of that presence and get us going again on the search for the Divine

Chapter 23 | Shifting Out of Separation into Oneness

outside of our bodies and in the future. We are still playing out the split between sacred and earthly life.

What if our bodies are just as sacred as our consciousness? Does the fact that our bodies are impermanent and temporary make them less divine? It is through our awareness and feeling sense of our body sensations that we move from beta brainwave frequencies into alpha and theta frequencies. It is through our bodies that we can feel and sense our Oneness with All-That-Is. What if our bodies, our daily lives *are* infused by the Highest Consciousness, God, Source? We know that to be true intellectually, and in our hearts and souls, but we might still need to update our subconscious separation programs to align with that truth.

So, here too, start being curious about your beliefs about your body. Beliefs about being in your daily life and in connection to the Divine. Listen to the messages of your subconscious—your thoughts, feelings, body sensations, and experiences. Find those beliefs that tell you why you can't live your daily life from Oneness.

. . . And then you can start clearing them, just like any other limiting belief.

The goal is not to clear all your limiting beliefs. A single lifetime might not be long enough to clear all your personal and collective limiting beliefs! The goal is to reduce them so you can make the shift to Oneness and your true being more easily.

It is not an improving but a shift that moves you from separation into Oneness.

Oneness is always here. It is only a thought or a belief that keeps you from feeling it. It is just a shift away.

It is not an improving but a shift that moves you from separation into Oneness.

It is:

- a shift from a beta to alpha and theta brainwave state.
- a shift from the logical thinking mind to the heart.
- a shift from knowledge to knowing.
- a shift from identifying with created forms to identifying with consciousness.

A light way to experience this shift is to ask yourself a "What if . . . " question:

"What if I am connected with everything?"

"What if I am one with everything?"

"What if all of me is sacred?"

"What if I am one with everything even with all my limiting beliefs?"

Then notice your body sensations, your energy, and your perception as the answer to these questions. To create a more lasting shift, you want to dissolve your separation beliefs.

Dissolving separation beliefs

Whether you believe you can't have a higher income or you can't live your daily life from Oneness, remember that both are limiting beliefs that were made up at some point in history and ended up with you.

> *Whether your limiting belief seems small or huge, the principles of how you dissolve that belief are the same.*

Whether your limiting belief seems small or huge, the principles of how you dissolve that belief are the same.

You can use the dissolving limiting beliefs process for separation beliefs in the same way you use it to dissolve limiting money beliefs. (See chapter 12, How to Tap to Dissolve Limiting Beliefs.)

Tapping example for dissolving a separation belief and shifting into Oneness

In the following tapping example, Sarah taps on a belief that she formed as a child by giving the adults' behaviour meaning. At the beginning of her tapping process it looks like Sarah is tapping on a "regular" childhood belief. It turns out the forming of this belief was crucial in her shifting out of her state of Oneness and into separation from her true being in childhood. The question that Sarah asks herself as she gets close to letting her limiting belief go is "Who am I then without this belief?" This question helps her reconnect to her true state of being that she lost as a young child.

1. Name and rate your limiting belief.

Sarah has known her belief for a long time: "Something is wrong with me."

She rates her belief and comes up with the number 9.

Part of her really wanted to shift this limiting belief. Another part of her was afraid to look at it more closely. Many months passed between her deciding to work on this belief and actually tapping on it.

Remember, you always want to tap on what is present in the moment. So, instead of tapping on the limiting belief right away, she tapped on what was present—the procrastination of actually tapping on the belief!

2. Create your set-up statement and tap it three times on the karate chop point.

Sarah comes up with this set-up statement: "Even though part of me does not want to tap on this, I choose to love and accept myself."

She taps her set-up statement three times on the karate chop point.

3. Tap on the belief or on feelings, body sensations, thoughts, memories, energies, images—any context that comes up around this belief.

Sarah taps, "I had this for so long." She feels a really strong emotional connection with this belief. She taps some more. "Who am I without this belief? Part of me feels really uncomfortable with the idea of not having it."

She reflects on how we form beliefs and how different parts of us—our intellect, our heart and soul, and our subconscious programming—see the truth of our beliefs differently.

She taps a round on this belief: "I've had this belief that something is wrong with me for a long, long time. It's from when I was quite little."

She does a check-in and says, "I feel a pull in my chest. Somehow this belief affects my heart. I also feel a tension, tightness, and restriction in my throat. This feeling is so familiar. I've had it for so long."

Sarah taps a whole round on these body sensations, feelings, and realizations from her check-in.

She talks about her experiences as a little child. "I always sensed and felt a lot from the time I was very young. And when I talked about it to the grown-ups, they didn't understand me. They didn't take me seriously. I sensed and knew that something wasn't right with the grown-ups. They were so closed off." She taps on this, one sentence at a time. Sarah starts to cry and sob. "They were so closed off. But they didn't know it. And they didn't understand what I was trying to tell them." She cries and then taps, "And at some point, I stopped sharing with them what I sensed and felt."

During her check-in Sarah becomes aware that something has changed in her throat. She taps on this. "Something is changing in my throat. There is a softness now on the right side, still tension and tightness, but it is held in softness."

4. Tap on how this belief came into your life.

a. Through making meaning of experiences growing up

Sarah continues tapping. "Because the grown-ups didn't understand what I sensed and noticed, I thought that there was something wrong with me. I started to believe that there was something wrong with me." She cries.

During her check-in she notices energy moving up and down in the centre of her body.

5. Tap on possible grief, regret, anger, sadness about having acquired and lived with this belief—the effect this belief has had on your life.

Sarah shares and taps, "Then when I was older, I started to work on myself. I still do that a lot! I am so tired and exhausted from it." She cries and taps, "Always this working on myself because I think something is wrong with me!"

6. Rate your belief again.

Sarah rates her belief again, and it is now a 5.

7. Tap on shifting the belief from being true to not true.

Sarah taps, "This belief—that there is something wrong with me—what if it's not actually true? What if the adults being so closed off was the reason they didn't understand me? What if there was actually nothing wrong with me? There was no one to explain that to me, so it makes sense that I started to believe that something was wrong with me. I realize now that this belief is not actually true."

During her check-in Sarah notices that the tension and tightness in her throat are gone. She notices an openness and relaxation there.

8. Tap on letting the limiting belief go.

Sarah is hesitant to let this belief go. Even though she realizes it's really not true, something in her feels a resistance to being without that belief. "Somehow I feel uncomfortable not having that belief."

Sarah taps, "Somehow I feel uncomfortable not having that belief. Because if that belief that there is something wrong with me is not true, who am I then?"

9. Tap on the supportive new belief.

Sarah notices that the energy in the centre of her body moves up and down again. She says and taps, "Then, I'm actually who I always was—love, light, and consciousness." Sarah stops tapping for a moment. She says, "The little child inside me is full of joy and agreement! She knows that this is true. She knows she is who she always was—love, light, and consciousness."

Sarah taps on that.

She does a check-in and notices an openness in her body. Her energy is high, and she feels full of joy.

Chapter 23 | Shifting Out of Separation into Oneness

She says and taps, "I am thinking about all the inner work I've done. All this inner work. Trying to find what was wrong with me and trying to change that. What if I don't have to do that anymore? If this belief is not true, there is nothing wrong with me! And I don't have to do all this inner work to improve what I thought was wrong with me. I could learn and improve and expand my skills for the love of it. Because it is fun, and it is joyful."

Sarah is so filled with joy. She wants to express it and feels like dancing.

A week later Sarah shared that she danced after finishing her tapping session, feeling openness, ease, flow, and joy in Oneness with the universe. She said she felt this openness and Oneness for several days after the tapping session. And then something challenging happened in her life and she lost the connection to her true self. After the challenge was taken care of, it was fairly easy for her to get back into being connected to her state of Oneness.

What happened?

Sarah recognized that when there is something on the outside that resembles the closed-off energy she experienced in the adults of her childhood, she loses her connection to her true self. She noticed she has the belief "Others and outside situations that have that closed-off energy can take me out of my connection to my true self." She realized she'd learned that belief when she was growing up.

Sarah went into the tapping process of dissolving this limiting belief. She moved fairly quickly into tapping **Step 7: Tap on shifting the belief from being true to not true.** She tapped, "What if it is not true? What if I can be and stay in my true state of being *and* deal with something challenging on the outside?"

Sarah realized that sometimes she needs her left-brain function and her beta brainwave skills to solve outside problems, and that in that moment she cannot *feel* her Oneness. She knows it does not mean it's not there. She is aware that she can keep the knowing of her true self and Oneness in her heart while she uses her linear intellect for outside tasks.

When you look at this tapping example, you'll notice that there are three closely connected beliefs:

"Something is wrong with me."

"I have to find what is wrong with me and fix it in order to be okay."

"Others can pull me out of my true state of being."

You might have had experiences as a small child that were similar to Sarah's. In *your* dissolving of separation beliefs, you might do as Sarah has done here and start with a "regular" childhood belief like:

"I am not good enough,"

"I am not wanted,"

"I am not lovable," or

"Something is wrong with me."

As you go through the layers of the experiences that created these beliefs and tap on untangling the meaning you made out of them, you'll find that ultimately every limiting belief is a belief that separates you from your true state of being!

You can also start with beliefs that state more directly your experience of separation like:

"Something in me believes that I am separate from others," or

Chapter 23 | Shifting Out of Separation into Oneness

"I have to be more pure, I have to be better to deserve being divine,"

or any other separation belief you hold. The more you clear your limiting beliefs, in particular your limiting beliefs of separation, the more you remove the illusion of separation between the different realms. The more you dissolve these beliefs, the easier it will be for you to shift into Oneness and to remain there longer.

So, you go through the same steps as you did for dissolving your other limiting beliefs.

You start with the set-up-statement, which might look like:

"Even though part of me believes that I am separate, I choose to love and accept myself."

"Even though I learned to believe that I am my body, I choose to be gentle and kind with myself."

"Even though I inherited this belief that my body is not sacred, I choose to be gentle and loving with myself."

Then you go through the sequence of tapping steps until you have dissolved the separation belief.

It might not dissolve completely at first, and you might have to go back and tap on it again. Remember the invisible collective website of our collective consciousness and collective unconsciousness and how we are all linked into it? All our human thoughts, feelings, stories, and beliefs are held there. All our collective separation beliefs are held there too. More and more people are aware of their money beliefs, their not-being-good-enough-beliefs, or not-being-lovable beliefs, and they tap on them! Not so many people tap on their separation beliefs yet. When you tap on dissolving *your* separation beliefs, you might notice that there is a strong pull on you from the separation beliefs held in the collective consciousness and unconsciousness. Notice this pull and continue dissolving your separation beliefs anyway. It might take a little longer, since the support from the collective field is not that strong yet. Be patient, gentle, and compassionate with yourself and all of humanity during this time of shifting beliefs.

As each one of us shifts and dissolves these old separation beliefs and as the information about those shifts gets posted on the collective website, it will become easier to dissolve separation beliefs—until personally and collectively we just don't believe them anymore! Just as we personally and collectively don't believe anymore that the Earth is flat!

What is supportive in this process of shifting into Oneness and living your daily life from there?

As with other needs, goals, and dreams in your life, become really clear about how you want to live. Bring your focus, attention, and intention to what you want. Create a clear picture and feeling sense of how you want to feel, be, and act when living from Oneness. Create an alive vision and feeling sense of how you want to be in that state with yourself, others, your immediate environment, and our planet. And then imagine what living from Oneness would mean for us collectively here on this planet. Write it down if you like.

- What are your beliefs about this vision? Find your beliefs that support your vision and the ones that limit you living these visions, goals, and dreams. Notice the messages from your subconscious that help you find these beliefs.

- Start to dissolve the limiting separation beliefs you found.

- Take action by using your doors and entranceways to the state of Oneness.

Chapter 23 | Shifting Out of Separation into Oneness

- Surround yourself with people, messages, books, and videos that support you in the shift—not because you need these to make that shift but because they can make it easier. We always influence each other through the information we carry visibly and invisibly.

- Your soul knows that you are connected to everything. When you anchor this knowing in your heart, you can go about your day trusting your knowing. You can use your beta brainwave skills when they are needed and still feel this knowing in your heart.

- Start changing your language. We use the words for "me," "you," "us" as synonyms for the words for our body. We say, for example, "I am thin" (or big). "You are tall" (or short). "We are young" (or old). This is a manifestation and expression of the inherited belief of "being our bodies." What we actually mean is "my, your, our body *looks* thin, big, tall, short, young, old."

    ○ How do you feel when you say, "*I* am young," "*I* am old," "*I* am tall," "*I* am short"?

    ○ How do you feel when you say, "*My body* is young," "*My body* is old," "*My body* is tall," "*My body* is short"?

    ○ How do different ways of saying it change your state of being?

Finally, imagine what kind of messages you would have needed when you were little to stay in the truth of who you are.

Imagine if you were greeted like this at birth: "Welcome, my love. I am so happy you are here. You are divine, and I see you. You are divine consciousness, and I am happy you chose this body to come into this life. I will do my best so that you can stay true to who you are. I'll always love you as who you are."

Of course, you would not have understood the words, but you would have felt the knowing in the other person. You would have felt the conscious, awake, and connected state of the person talking to you.

And imagine that as you were growing up, you were spoken to like this:

"Be true to yourself. Stay true to yourself. I will support you in this."

"Do you remember where you were before you were born into this body?"

"Many people on this planet believe in worthy and unworthy, lovable and unlovable, and they lose their connection to love and to their source. Don't believe them."

"We have given you this name, and you can change it if you notice, feel, or sense that it is not right for you (anymore)."

"You are divine and always will be. You are always in communication with the Divine in you. This is how you co-create in this life. You always have choices in your life, and we support you in your true choices."

"Your body is beautiful, no matter what anybody says. Your body is sacred."

"You are unique and special. There is no one like you. You are special in your uniqueness. You were made for this life exactly right. You are needed and wanted exactly as you are. We love you unconditionally."

"Everyone is unique on this planet. Everyone is an expression of the Divine, Highest Consciousness. You are connected to everyone and everything on this planet."

CHAPTER 23 | SHIFTING OUT OF SEPARATION INTO ONENESS

"Notice and listen to your feelings. They show you what to think, what to do, what to follow, and what to avoid. Your feelings connect you to your needs. Your needs are part of the creative process. Your needs are beautiful. Allow them to guide you in creating your life experiences."

Imagine you were spoken to like this. Imagine these were messages you got growing up. You probably would not be reading this book—or maybe you would be reading it in History class.

Which messages would *you* have liked to hear?

Choose a few and say them out loud to yourself, then notice:

- your body sensations,
- your feelings, and
- your thoughts.

Imagine that when you were born and when you grew up you were recognized as your soul, as a spiritual being, as consciousness who came into this body. Imagine you grew up with these messages.

You would not have learned separation beliefs, and so you wouldn't need to dissolve any in order to live in Oneness.

You would live your daily life, this earthly life, from sacredness, from Oneness, from living your truth and your knowing. You would live in the knowing that you are infinite consciousness, expressing here in your daily life through impermanent forms and experiences.

Like children who are pretending that their leg is broken, and the game is to heal the broken leg. They play and pretend all different ways of how to heal their leg. And then their mother calls them for supper and they say, "That was fun." They get up to go to supper, knowing that their leg was never broken. There was nothing that needed to be healed. They were complete all along.

You would know this earthly life as a game, a play, a story that you are playing with others. You would know that your life is a made-up reality. You would not identify with your inner and outer creations or judge anything as worthy or unworthy. Instead you would feel yourself as observing consciousness with unconditional love for All-That-Is. Your limiting beliefs do not exist in that reality of consciousness, and therefore you would not need "dissolving" in this realm. You would not need any aspects of this play to prove your worthiness, your lovability, your inclusion, or your good-enoughness. In this reality you would not need to find or to prove your sacredness.

You would live fully present in your body, feet on the Earth, co-creating consciously, anchored in Highest Consciousness. You would know the Field of Infinite Possibilities and use its laws to co-create with. You would enjoy the magic that happens when you live from there. You would not identify with your co-creations and yet would still do your best to co-create well. The limiting beliefs would be gone, and your needs taken care of.

You would feel a lightness, expansiveness, flow, inclusiveness, and unconditional love, and Oneness with All-That-Is.

And in your "outer" life, things, events, and circumstances would seem to shift effortlessly into the right places, connections, movements, and flow.

You would just enjoy the play—creating beauty, expressing love and caring, being in harmony and peace with each other and everything around you.

You would allow yourself to listen to the messages of your soul and the Highest Consciousness.

Sound like a fairytale? Yes, it does.

CHAPTER 23 | SHIFTING OUT OF SEPARATION INTO ONENESS

And even though we can think and imagine this, most of us, and humanity collectively, are still far away from living this possibility.

But just as you are making and have made changes in your personal life that seemed far away from your ideal, you can do that as well in the collective areas of our lives.

What would living in oneness mean to you? How would that look like, feel like? Relating to your personal life, your family, your work, the people where you live? What would be different for you in the whole of humanity, on our planet? Would it be world peace? Would it be equal worthiness of all people and beings? Enough water and food for everyone? Balanced climate? Would it be fairly shared properties and money? Would it be understanding and emotionally intelligent communication among people? Would it be compassion and empathy for each other and healing of traumas? Would it be . . . ?

Feel and connect with that which *you* feel drawn to.

Can you stand up for this vision out of an inner feeling and sensing of Oneness? And can you hold your vision in this mindset in the midst of the discrepancy between your inner vision and how our world is right now? That is not easy at all! Most of the time we get pulled out of our being in Oneness by the traumatic events and injustices in our world.

Remember for a moment the set-up statement at the beginning of your tapping rounds. "Even though . . . (here you said out loud a challenge in your life) . . . I can be gentle and loving with myself." And in the same way you can approach collective challenges and injustices of varying degrees. You can hold them in understanding, compassion and from a place of unconditional love. Because all these collective injustices and challenges in our world are the effect of unhealed traumas, that happened in the past of our human story.

And so, you can start tapping on your feelings, thoughts, reactions to these collective challenges and traumas in our world, holding yourself in empathy, compassion and loving energy. And when all your feelings of sadness, fear, anger, frustration, hopelessness ... feel heard, seen, understood and validated, then look for your inner and outer steps in areas of the world to which you feel drawn and called to.

Find these steps from your state of Oneness and not from an energy of resisting and fighting against. (See: "Set-up statement pg ...) Acceptance does not mean not taking action. It also doesn't mean that you can't be against something and speak up. It means, that your speaking up and your actions come from an energy of understanding, compassion and a love that holds all – your actions arise from your presence in Oneness.

What will your contribution be? What are your skills and gifts that you can give to the earth, humanity, to nature, to all beings on our planet?

- Become really clear about your goals and dreams for this reality of Oneness in our world,
- find the limiting beliefs that keep you from bringing your skills and gifts forward to realize these goals and dreams,
- clear those limiting beliefs, and
- then take inner and outer action.

What would you like to change for yourself personally? What in your family, at your workplace, the school of your children, in your environment, for the people in your community and what would you like to contribute globally that meets your vision of Oneness?

And in this process, remember to honour yourself in the way you experience this journey. It is your unique and beautiful expression of consciousness as your life.

Chapter 23 | Shifting Out of Separation into Oneness

There are countless ways to find the path back to living Heaven on Earth, back to Oneness, and to living your life from the knowing, the clarity, and love of your soul.

Your journey is special and unique. Take from others and from this book what is inspiring and helpful for you and leave what is not. Even though our human beliefs are shared, there is no other life exactly like yours!

Appendix 1: Universal Human Needs List[5]

Physical Well-Being
Air
Water
Food
Sleep
Shelter
Movement
Health
Touch

Connection
Acceptance
Belonging
Inclusion
Consideration
Support
Respect
Appreciation
Communication
Cooperation
Compassion
Mutuality
Companionship
Community
Closeness
Love
Intimacy
Affection
Empathy
Consistency

To be seen
To be understood
To understand

Peace
Safety
Security
Stability
Justice
Fairness
Harmony
Trust
Equality
Reliability
Honesty
Authenticity
Integrity
Order

Autonomy
Freedom
Choice
Independence
Self-expression
Inspiration
Spontaneity

Fun
Imagination
Adventure
Humour
Laughter
Relaxation

Happiness
Joy
Calm
Grounding
Presence
Ease
Balance
Passion
Beauty

Meaning
Awareness
Consciousness
Purpose
Gratitude

Growth
Discovery
Creativity
Learning
Participation
Stimulation
Clarity
Understanding
Contribution
To matter
Competence
Challenge
Capability
Effectiveness
Mourning
Hope

---

5 Drawn from the Center for Nonviolent Communication's Needs List (2005). www.cnvc.org

Appendix 2: Feelings List[6]

Feelings When Needs Are Met

Happy	**Alive**	Astonished
Joyful	Invigorated	Absorbed
Blissful	Stimulated	Amazed
Delighted	Animated	Eager
Joyous	Energetic	Thrilled
Glad	Refreshed	Intrigued
Cheerful	Recharged	**Safe**
Pleased	**Confident**	Secure
Affectionate	Calm	Grounded
Warm	Content	**Grateful**
Tender	Relaxed	Appreciative
Loving	Peaceful	Thankful
Open-hearted	**Excited**	Fulfilled
Present	Fascinated	Touched
Compassionate	Inspired	Moved
Quiet	Amazed	**Encouraged**
Curious	Enthusiastic	Hopeful
Interested	Exuberant	Relieved
Centred	Passionate	Optimistic

---

6 Drawn from the Center for Nonviolent Communication's Feelings list (2005). www.cnvc.org

Feelings When Needs Are Not Met

Afraid	Mad	**Disconnected**
Scared	Enraged	Lonely
Terrified	**Annoyed**	Distant
Shocked	Frustrated	Bored
Concerned	Impatient	Indifferent
Worried	Irritable	Empty
Nervous	Resentful	Numb
Apprehensive	Bitter	**Pain**
Fearful	**Aversion**	Grief
Petrified	Appalled	Broken-hearted
Guarded	Disgusted	Aching
Panicked	Bothered	Agony
Sad	Repulsed	Regretful
Hurt	**Confused**	Remorseful
Upset	Uncertain	**Agitated**
Unhappy	Hesitant	Restless
Withdrawn	Ambivalent	Disturbed
Depressed	Conflicted	Troubled
Despair	Disoriented	Unsettled
Gloomy	Puzzled	**Ashamed**
Miserable	Torn	Embarrassed
Hopeless	**Overwhelmed**	Self-conscious
Disappointed	Distressed	**Tired**
Discouraged	Discouraged	Exhausted
Angry	**Anxious**	Depleted
Furious	Insecure	Burned out
Hateful	Tense	**Yearning**
Hostile	Uncomfortable	Longing

Appendix 3: Road Map for Navigating the Trigger Response and Getting to the Gems

Become aware of your triggered state	Recognize, become aware that you are triggered
	Know your trigger responses
	- notice your body symptoms
	- notice your feelings
	- notice your thoughts
	Communicate that you are triggered, if appropriate
Come to a calm state	Create time and space for yourself, away from the triggering situation and person you got triggered by
	- go outside
	- take a bathroom break
	Take your focus off the other person and bring it to yourself
	Come to calm when by yourself
	- feel your feet on the ground
	- take deep breaths into your belly

- hold yourself in compassion, give yourself empathy, verbally and nonverbally
- do some physical exercise
- use EFT to calm your emotions
- engage in activities that are caring for yourself and your surroundings

Find the gems	Identify the needs that were not met for you in the triggering situation (use the needs list in Appendix 1) Find and identify your thoughts and your beliefs about the unmet needs
Shift the limiting beliefs	State your limiting beliefs Dissolve the limiting beliefs - use EFT - use the "What-if process"

Appendix 4: Tapping Protocol for Dissolving Limiting Beliefs

Even though a tapping journey of dissolving a limiting belief most of the time follows organically the steps outlined here, sometimes it skips a step or comes back to a previous one. For your own tapping process use this protocol as a guideline. Most importantly, follow your own feeling sense which step to go to. Your feeling sense is informed by your subconscious.

I. Starting point if you don't know your limiting belief

1. Create a statement about your feelings, your body sensations, your thoughts, a situation, a trigger, an unfulfilled need, dream, or goal.

2. Create your set-up statement and tap it three times on the karate chop point.

3. Continue tapping rounds on points 2-9, using statements about feelings, experiences, body sensations, thoughts, memories of situations, unfulfilled needs, dreams, or goals.

4. Do check-ins after each round. Continue tapping on the statement you started with or use statements that hold the information from your check-ins.

5. Do the tapping while holding curiosity about your underlying belief. When you are ready, ask yourself, "What must I believe that I feel/sense/think/experience this?"

6. Find the underlying belief.

Once you know your underlying limiting belief go to the steps under II. Starting point if you know your limiting belief.

II. Starting point if you know your limiting belief

1. Name and rate your limiting belief.

2. Create your set-up statement and tap it three times on the karate chop point.

3. Tap on the belief or on feelings, body sensations, thoughts, memories, energies, images—any context that comes up around this belief. Do check-ins after your rounds. Use the information that comes up in your check-ins for your next statements.

4. Tap on how this belief came into your life through:

   a. making meaning of experiences growing up, or

   b. absorbing and/or inheriting the belief growing up.

5. Tap on possible grief, regret, anger, sadness about having acquired and lived with this belief—the effect this belief has had on your life.

6. Rate your belief again. If it is 5 or higher, go to A-E (see page 150).

If it is 5 or lower, go to step 7.

7. Tap on shifting the belief from being true to not true. Go back to A-E if necessary.

8. Tap on letting the limiting belief go. Go back to A-E if necessary.

9. Tap on the supportive, new belief. Go back to A-E if necessary.

10. Test the result.

Acknowledgements

I remember sitting at a picnic table in one of the most beautiful parks on the BC coast and drafting out the chapters of this book. When I reflect on it, though, I realize this book did not start there. It started with living decades of my life becoming more conscious of when I lived in limitation and when I was free of it. I am grateful for my soul, for all the times it nudged me out of those limitations and kept me learning, unlearning, and shifting. But it didn't even start with me or my experiences. It started somewhere way back in history.

I am grateful for the people who came before me and who lived in times of more limitations than we live in today.

I am grateful for all the people I learned from and who guided and supported me on my path. Their books, workshops, counselling and healing sessions, online teachings, and words of wisdom in our shared distant or recent past helped me find and articulate what I share with you in this book.

I am grateful for all the support from the unseen realm.

I didn't have big plans to write a book. It just wanted to be written, and I agreed and surrendered to it. What a team effort it was! Writing a book in my second language was a special journey. I learned that English readers don't cherish sentences that are half a page long. And I learned some quirky terminology about English punctuation and typography. I am deeply grateful for all the skilled writers and editors who made this book better for English readers, round after round: Bessie Gantt, Dacia Moss, Chuck Lazer, and Lesley Cameron. I couldn't have done it without you!

My scribbled diagrams and visions for illustrations were brought to life by Marian Dessa, Bernadette Mertens-McAllister, Jan Westendorp, and Angela Fraser. I am grateful to Angela Fraser for making the creation of the book cover such a joyful collaboration. A big thank-you to Jan Westendorp for turning the manuscript into a real book. Thank you all for your amazing skills.

I am grateful for all the feedback that you all gave me so readily and open-heartedly. "How does this look?" "How does this read to you?" "Does this make sense to you?" You never got tired of answering these questions for me. I especially want to thank my core feedback team of Avery, Amrei, and Barry Hunter; Dacia Moss and Chuck Lazer; Carola Heydemann; Sheri Standen; and my amazing friends in my neighbourhood.

I thank my family in Canada and in Germany for celebrating each accomplishment in this writing journey with me.

I am deeply grateful to all of you who have worked with me over the years in counselling and healing sessions. I feel honoured that you chose me to walk some steps of your journey with you. I learned a lot from you. Your courage, commitment, and growth give me hope and trust that together, as humanity, we can create a better world.

www.ingramcontent.com/pod-product-compliance
Lightning Source LLC
Chambersburg PA
CBHW072047110526
44590CB00018B/3072